4.95

LESBIANS TALK T

LESBIANS TALK

Trans gender

Zachary I Nataf

Scarlet Press

306.76

Acknowledgements

To the vision of the women at Scarlet Press for anticipating the impact transgender is going to have on the lesbian community and their courage in creating a space for the debates to begin.

Thanks to Liz Gibbs and Avis Lewallen at Scarlet for their encouragement and belief in my contributions to the debate.

Thanks to Ivor Delafield for the use of the office and computer.

My thanks to all the contributors, especially Kate Bornstein, Leslie Feinberg, Riki Ann Wilchins, Judith Halberstam and David Harrison for helping to raise my transgender consciousness.

To Cherry Smyth for her insight, wisdom and humanity.

To Steven Whittle for his intelligent and compassionate commitment to the community.

To Nasreen Memon, whose effort to transcend being lesbian matched my effort to transcend being a transsexual man in order to share queer bodies and a special love. These efforts have had a profound value for me.

Published in 1996 by Scarlet Press
5 Montague Road, London, E8 2HN

British Library Cataloguing-in-Publication Data
A catalogue record for this book is available from the British Library
ISBN 1 85727 008 8

20027225

Series editor: Liz Gibbs
Cover design: Pat Kahn
Produced for Scarlet Press by
Chase Production Services, Chipping Norton
Typeset from author's disk by
Stanford DTP Services, Milton Keynes
Printed in the EC by J.W. Arrowsmith, Bristol

Contents

9   Terminology, classification and boundaries

17   New genders and pansexualities

35   Lesbians and transgender since the transsexual empire

54   The future: the postmodern lesbian body and transgender trouble

60   Bibliography

63   Glossary

64   Contacts

Author statement

I became aware of my gender identity conflict at the age of five. By the time I was ten I realised that my friends thought I was crazy when I insisted that there had been some mix up in the womb and that I should have been a boy. I quickly learned to keep silent and hide it from the people around me until I confessed my desire for sex-change surgery to my first girlfriend at the age of 16. But I still didn't believe it would ever be possible, so I tried to forget. I lived as a butch lesbian for 20 years, a very effective strategy for coping with my gender dysphoria before I was able to believe that I could live as a transgendered person without falling off the social map of what is permitted to exist. I am emerging directly into a transgender community, but retain ties with the lesbian community which had proved to be fertile ground for subverting patriarchal gender norms. What had been missing for me for all those years was to see representations of transgender people, especially FTMs, and to hear their stories. It was very important to me to be involved with producing this book, in an effort to clear up some misconceptions about TG people and, to begin to represent some of the different ways of being gendered and allow for voices to be heard, which are too often still not being taken seriously even by the lesbian and gay community, sometimes with fatal consequences. I sometimes wonder whatever happened to an MTF lesbian lover I had in New York when I was 19. If you are still out there, Vanessa, I hope you will read this book with pride.

Contributors

Rosemary Auchmuty is principal lecturer in law at the University of Westminster and a lesbian feminist

Inge Blackman is a filmmaker who has directed films for Channel 4 and Carlton TV, and who lusts after spunky femmes

Kate Bornstein, author of *Gender Outlaw*, is a playwright, performer and transgendered dyke

Caroline is MTF transsexual and a femme lesbian

Christie Elan-Cane is a third gender activist and 'pissed off with being treated as a freak'

Leslie Feinberg, author of *Stone Butch Blues*, is a transgender activist, lesbian transgenderist

Gerry is a black bisexual man, former FTM transsexual

Della Grace describes herself as a hermaphrodyke, anarcho-photographer, who is currently embarked on a splendid gender adventure

Paula Graham is a writer, lecturer in cultural studies and dyke

Alison Gregory is lesbian, former editor of the *Pink Paper* and currently a broadcast journalist for the BBC

Judith Halberstam is a writer and lecturer in literature at the University of California at San Diego, identifying as stone butch and transgendered

David Harrison is a writer, playwright and performer and FTM transsexual, pansexual man

Susan Hayward works in the media and describes herself as a lesbian top femme

Josephine Asher is a senior residential social worker and black MTF transsexual who identifies as lesbian

Kacha is an actor, musician and East Asian lesbian

Roz Kaveney is a publisher's reader, SF writer and critic, contributing editor of the *Encyclopaedia of Fantasy*, *New Statesman* reviewer and MTF TS, lesbian identified feminist and Liberty activist

Annette Kennerley is a northern, working-class dyke mother and filmmaker, an unstereotypical femme and nearly 40

Martin, a teacher in his previous incarnation, currently works in science research and is a volunteer counsellor, gay man, FTM transsexual who has lived with his lover for ten years

Hilary McCollum works for the Women's Unit of a London borough council, is a radical lesbian feminist and a member of Campaign Against Pornography

Spike Pittsberg has been a writer of journalism, fiction and pornography for a quarter of a century. She is also a queer ballroom, Latin American and country and western dancer

Cherry Smyth is an Irish dyke writer, journalist, and curator, living in London

Dr Steven Whittle is co-author of *Transvestism, Transsexualism and the Law*, lecturer in law in Manchester, Press for Change activist, founder of the FTM Network, TS man and father of two

Riki Ann Wilchins, a New York transgender activist, founder of Transsexual Menace, signs her e-mail: 'just your average straight white guy with a cunt who digs lesbian chicks like me'

Terminology, classification and boundaries

Transsexualism is for many people something that became imaginable and indeed came into existence in the 1950s when the international media sensationalised the story of the male-to-female (MTF) 'sex change' of American Christine Jorgensen. Since then a few autobiographies of male-to-females – Jan Morris, Renée Richards and more recently Caroline Cossey – gave people the idea that while transsexuality wasn't a one off, it was certainly a rare phenomenon, made possible only because of modern technology and something only done by men. Only recently has the existence of female-to-male (FTM) transsexuals been recognised by the popular media.

Cross-gender identity and behaviour have been known and recorded since antiquity. From Aristotle to the Middle Ages, the Renaissance and the Enlightenment in the eighteenth century, gender was the key category and biological sex was fluid and mutable. In *Making Sex: Body and Gender from the Greeks to Freud* Thomas Laqueur describes how the 'one-sex model' – which held that a woman's body was a variation on rather than a different sex to a man's – gave way to the 'two-sex model' in the nineteenth century. The institutions controlling sexual behaviours, especially that which departed from societal norms, shifted from the church's jurisdiction to that of the state, and thus came a shift from sins against God to 'crimes against nature'. From the 1840s legal institutions looked to medical science for definitions and explanations, ranging from perversion to pathology, with debates about whether the causes of such behaviour were innate and genetic (biological) or the result of rearing and environment (of the mind). These politically powerful systems attempted to explain and to cure. They had no effect on the continued occurrence of cross-gender expression, but did affect the way transgendered people were perceived and treated. Early case histories focused on errors in gender assignment at birth, inversion (later known as homosexuality) and 'psychic' hermaphroditism, including transsexualism.

Women had cross-dressed and passed as men throughout history, primarily to escape poverty and social restrictions. The majority of these women were heterosexual and usually went back to live as women when they found the right man. Fewer cross-lived because they were hermaphrodite, lesbians, or dissatisfied with or disagreed with their gender assignment. With the exception of François Timoleon de Choisy, known as the the Abbé de Choisy (1644–1724), men cross-living without detection was rare until the nineteenth century. The consolidation of homosexuality as an identity and lifestyle grew out of the 'Molly clubs' and popular masked balls of the eighteenth century which became safe places where men cross-dressed and experimented with gender reversal publicly, reflecting the emergence of personal civil liberties. Although some non-homosexual men who cross-dressed were fetishists, others were what was to become known as transvestite. There were also those who were not only rebelling against the constraints of masculinity and the male role, but were dissatisfied with their gender assignment too.

In the Middle Ages and Renaissance, canon and civil law designated her-maphrodites as those in whom the two sexes were juxtaposed. It was for the person who named the child, father or godfather, to determine her/his sex. On reaching the age of marriage, the individual was free to decide whether or not to continue living in the assigned sex. Once the decision was declared it had to be kept to, under pain of breaking the sodomy laws. But by the nineteenth century a hermaphrodite's identity was determined by medical, civil and church law (see Foucault, *Herculine Barbin*).

We can see from this that perceptions of gender are historically specific and change from one historical period to another. R.W. Connell in *Gender and Power: Society, the Person and Sexual Politics* argues for a whole new gender category to be constructed, as with the emergence of 'the homosexual' in the late nineteenth century, and perhaps 'the transsexual' now.

In 1886, in *Psychopathia Sexualis*, Dr Richard von Krafft-Ebing wrote:

the physical and psychical characteristics of inverted sexuality are so plentiful that a mistake cannot occur. Psychically they consider themselves to belong to the opposite sex. They act, walk, gesticulate and behave in every way exactly as if they were persons of the sex which they simulate.

Krafft-Ebing coined the term 'gynandry' to describe the gender identity disorder which appears to correspond to twentieth-century instances of FTM transsexuals.

Surgical intervention in sex conversion began to appear at the end of the nineteenth century. The earliest known case concerned Sophie Hedwig, whose genitalia were masculinised in 1882, enabling him to officially change sex and thus become Herman Karl, though details of the procedure are incomplete. The physician and writer Alberta Lucille/Alan Hart is considered one of the first verified FTM transsexuals. Having begun psychotherapy because of a phobia for loud noises, Alberta ended the analysis in 1917, obtained a hysterectomy, changed identity to that of a man and married. The account of the sex change of MTF Lili Elbe in 1930 is described in a book edited by Niels Hoyers, *Man into Woman*, published in 1933. The well-known Danish painter had started life as Einar Wegener, who was convinced a female twin shared his body. He visited a number of doctors, whose diagnosis ranged from homosexuality to speculation that he had the rudiments of female gonads within his body. Wegener then went to Berlin, where a surgeon removed his penis and testicles.

Elbe secured a passport in her new name and her earlier marriage was declared null and void by the king of Denmark. She returned to Berlin to have a vagina constructed but died soon after the operation (Vern and Bonnie Bullough, *Cross Dressing, Sex, and Gender*).

The first MTF surgeries involved only excision of the testicles (an orchiectomy) and amputation of the penis (a penectomy), with no attempt to construct a vagina or clitoris. Later efforts used a section of the intestine within a cavity created in the pelvic area, with limited success, until the 1960s when Dr George Burou of Casablanca developed a surgical technique which involved inverting the tissue of the scraped-out skin of the penis to create the walls of the vagina. Also significant in the medicalisation of transsexualism was the developing field of endocrinology in the 1920s, with the isolation and syn-thesising of the sex hormones, testosterone and oestrogen. In 1937 hormones became generally available as tablets or through injections. In 1949 the British aristocrat Michael Dillon, born Laura in 1915, was the first FTM transsexual to have full sex reassignment surgery (SRS) – except for a hysterectomy – with hormone therapy. Dillon's phalloplasty was carried out by plastic surgeon Sir Harold Gillies, who had developed this surgery for men who had lost their genitals in the war or in accidents, or for those born with ambiguous genitalia. The grafting of Dillon's neo-phallus and scrotum required 13 operations over four years. Sixty years after the first ever surgically constructed penis in 1936, the technique remains experimental (Liz Hodgkinson, *Michael, Née Laura*).

The state of the art?

Popularly referred to as sex-change surgery, the medical technology of hormone therapy and plastic surgery is currently known by the conceptually laden term sex reassignment surgery or gender reassignment surgery. Psychiatrists are 'gatekeepers' to the treatment. Unlike any other condition, the request for access to SRS is the only diagnostic criterion.

This distinct diagnostic category was formulated by endocrinologist Dr Harry Benjamin after the Jorgensen case in his book *The Transsexual Phenomenon* (1966). According to this, transsexuals not only had a cross-gender identity but also a persistent and sustained desire for surgical conversion.

In 1980 transsexualism was officially recognised as an illness in the third edition of the American Psychiatric Association's *Diagnostic and Statistical Manual of Mental Disorders* (DSM), from which homosexuality had been removed only in 1973. The definition was revised in 1987. Although it will be further revised for the next edition, transgender activists are lobbying for the depathologising of transsexuality within the Association and DSM.

Treatment following the *Standards of Care* drawn up by Walker et al. in 1979 includes assessment using psychotherapy and a series of body image, personality and sex-role evaluation tests. This is followed by a period of living in role, known as the 'real-life test', usually beginning three months before hormone therapy and continued for at least a year before the first stages of surgery are recommended.

Living in role successfully generally involves having a job and a relationship in which the client is accepted in her/his new gender identity. Hormones are indispensable in allowing this to be achieved, inducing the secondary sex characteristics and annihilating some of the characteristics of the natal sex. For MTFs beard growth requires removal by electrolysis, the voice pitch does not change significantly, but breast development occurs over a few years and balding ceases, testicles shrink, ejaculations cease, the libido reduces and erections become increasingly difficult to achieve. For FTMs there is no significant reduction in breast size but the voice deepens, body and facial hair grows, male pattern balding may begin, menstruation ceases, muscles become denser, libido increases, the clitoris elongates and enlarges by up to 4–8 centimetres; and, although I have read no reports of this, from my own experience there may be increased activity of the prostate/paraurethral gland and ejaculation. Because of the removal of testes and ovaries following SRS, transsexuals must receive lifelong hormone replacement to maintain sex characteristics and health.

If a person seeking SRS is married, gender programmes require a divorce before recommending genital surgery and a change of civil status, where that is permitted. In most places such a marriage cannot be legally maintained.

Numerous international follow-up studies reveal an extremely high success rate for gender reassignment, an average of 97–100 per cent in FTMs and 87–90 per cent in MTFs. The treatment is reported to not only alleviate the gender dysphoria but to turn to gender euphoria in some cases. From clients who reported depression, anxiety and, often, attempted suicide, the resulting mental peace and adjustment are notable even if they are not completely satisfied with the aesthetic outcome of the surgery. Regrets that are reported are usually due to surgery being unavailable, or to serious surgical complications and poor results.

In Britain only 2–3 per cent of FTMs have phalloplasties. It is estimated that 2,000–3,000 have been carried out by two surgeons, currently costing £20,000–30,000, with generally poor results. A good phalloplasty would give a client a neo-phallus that looks like a penis, the ability to urinate while standing, and the ability to have penetrative sex. The luxury of erotic sensation incurs further expense, with an operation transplanting a nerve from the forearm. Various devices are used to achieve an erection, while silicone balls simulating testicles are implanted in a scrotum formed from the labia. In the US some of the best work is done by a Dr Gilbert but the process costs $200,000. Many Americans have metoidioplasties (meaning 'changing towards male genitals'). This releases the clitoral penis and costs around $25,000–30,000. The major US specialist in MTF surgery is Stanley Biber in Colorado, who has performed more than 2,000 operations. In Europe the Swiss surgeon Meyer is known for both MTF and FTM surgeries, with a vaginoplasty costing £20,000. In the Netherlands, funded by the national health system, Dr Joris

Hage has responded enthusiastically to the challenge of phalloplasty and has had very good results.

Transgender across culture

Outside the West, an intermediate gender status or third gender category with a special social function exists in many cultures in a variety of forms. The best-known are the Native American berdache and the hijras of India.

These instances suggest the arbitrariness of using categories of male and female based on anatomical morphology as the sole criterion for gendered classification systems, because in some cultures it is gender roles, not anatomy, which are the central constituent factor of gender. Although gender everywhere is part of a classification system which makes it socially intelligible, anatomy is not the 'natural', universal determinant of gender.

The Gay American Indians History Project has begun documenting accounts of the diverse social roles of Native American transgendered men and women of many nations, collectively referred to by anthropologists as berdache. Since the 1600s explorers and anthropologists have recorded the existence of 'male' berdache in 150 North American societies and of 'female' berdache in half of these. The word berdache, a misnomer which says more about the observers than what they actually witnessed, is from the Persian 'bardag', synonymous with catamite, meaning a boy kept by a man as his courtesan.

Data indicates that berdache sexual behaviour was variable. They participated in both casual and long-term relationships with partners who were usually non-berdache and of the same biological sex. Those who were bi- or heterosexual were most often those who reached berdache status as adults after a spiritual experience in a dream or vision (Will Roscoe, 'How to Become a Berdache').

In India, one of the world's oldest civilisations, transgender representation and expression have a 2,500 year old history in religious mythology, literature and art, as well as in medical literature and social roles and identities. The Ayurvedic medical teachings, which originated as an oral tradition dating back to the second millennium BC, were set down in written form between 600 BC and AD 100. Naranarishandou, the umbrella term used for various different sexual groups, translates as man (nara) woman (nari), unable to produce progeny (shandou). The juxtaposition of nara and nari signifies a womanish man or mannish woman, while the lack of progeny may be attributed to a lack of copulatory behaviour rather than sterility (John Money, 'Transsexualism and Homosexuality in Sanskrit').

In modern Hindi the word is rendered as 'hijra' but, like transgender, this covers a vast range of cross-gender expression that includes intersex people, assigned as both men and women (who fail to menstruate); transvestites; homosexuals; and those who fit the Western diagnostic description of transsexual. In the eighteenth and nineteenth centuries, surgical removal of the penis, testes and scrotum was available within the community and people who had this done lived fulltime in the role of women. Others in the hijra community included those seeking a religious transformation and rebirth as devotees of the Mother Goddess Bahuchara Mata and prostitutes seeking refuge, both of whom may have had a more ambivalent view of the sexual surgery. In fact the cultural meaning of the emasculation was to transform people not into women but into hijras: 'scared, erotic, female men' (Serena Nanda, 'Hijras'). It is the ambiguous gender identity within a socially delineated third sex caste, 'neither man nor woman', which characterises the hijras.

With the advent of colonial rule the British were able to stigmatise the hijras' traditional position, removing their state protection and introducing laws that criminalised emasculation, which were incorporated into the criminal code of independent India. But the laws do not seem to deter the secret practising of emasculations. And although Indian culture traditionally recognises and validates 'many different ways of being human', recent government punishment of their practices has begun to stigmatise the hijra community (Serena Nanda, 'Hijras').

Legal definitions

The terms sex and gender are used to distinguish biological differences from those arising from social, cultural and psychological systems. Their relationship is both motivated and arbitrary in that biological sex is universally used as a system of social diffentiation, but historically and across cultures gender is not directly derived from biology and is culturally relative, stemming primarily from political, economic, moral, religious and legal domains.

Sex determination is complex. Seven variables have been identified: chromosomal sex, gonadal sex, hormonal sex, internal reproductive organs – uterus and prostate gland – external genitals, assigned sex and gender role (Katherine O'Donovan, 'Transsexual Troubles'). It seems the more complex the determinants of biological sex have become with scientific investigation, the less reliable sex is in indicating gender, so genitals remain the primary factor in assigning and attributing sex despite the presence of contradictory biological evidence. Often gender does not correspond exactly to sex and sometimes it is even more difficult to determine sex from interrelated but incongruent biological factors.

Although most people with intersex conditions (hermaphroditism or pseudo-hermaphroditism) born now are medically 'corrected' soon after birth and before their birth certificates are filed, they make up an estimated 4 per cent of all births: 216 million people worldwide (Aimée Waddington, 'Herms, Ferms, Merms and the Biopower of the Surgical Shoehorn'). For those whose families resisted medical intervention, or whose condition only became known at puberty, or who decide that the doctors have made an error in their assignment and they are transsexual, the legal situation in Britain regarding the treatment of people who do not fit into the two-sex model has not changed since the 1860s.

Although modern medical research and theory suggest that the categories of woman and man are not in fact biologically opposite or closed, but that people fall somewhere along a continuum, legal reasoning is based on the classification of persons and acts and of biological sex as closed.

A significant case in the UK, Corbett v. Corbett (1970), concerned a couple who had married with the knowledge that the female partner, April Ashley, was MTF transsexual. When the marriage failed, the male partner wished to declare it null and void on the grounds that both parties were male. Mr Justice Ormrod ruled that the law should determine sex based on the congruence of 'the chromosomal, gonadal and genital tests' and that 'the biological sexual constitution of an individual is fixed at birth (at the latest) and cannot be changed either by natural development of organs of the opposite sex or by medical or surgical means'.

Appealing for compassion as well as logic, Ormrod's critics argued that since the chromosome pattern can never be changed it should be ignored; and that the genital test should be based on the actual postoperative state of the genitals, with the category or apparent sex of an individual decided according to the congruence of genitals, gender identity and gender roles (Katherine O'Donovan, 'Transsexual Troubles'). Although Ormrod's ruling that Ashley was a man was intended to apply only to marriage, it has been used on every occasion since then when a transsexual's sex has had to be legally determined. Since that 1970 ruling, transsexuals in the UK have been unable to have their birth or death certificates amended or to marry.

Genetic and other theories

In the current theories of the 'cause' of transsexualism, gender identity is seen as a complex interaction of genetic predisposition, physiological factors and the process of socialisation. Both nature and nurture play a part and each side of the nature/nurture divide has its proponents. Because every known society (historically and cross-culturally) has produced cross-gendered people, there is strong evidence to support a genetic influence. The physiological argument is that prenatal hormones influence the neural pathways and neuroendocrine links between the hypothalamus (the part of the brain that controls sex drive), the pituitary gland and other endocrine glands. These pathways, which later control the production of hormones, affect gender and sexual behaviour (Milton Diamond, 'Human Sexual Development').

Of all the factors involved, sex assignment and rearing have a stronger impact than any biological tendency might. Currently it is believed that the critical period of gender imprinting, which starts at birth, is 18 months. By this age gender role is thought to be established. Psychotherapist and researcher Robert Stoller argues that there is no evidence to support theories of genetic or biochemical abnormalities in most transsexuals. This is not to say there may not be biological pointers. Most recently research has concentrated on the hypothalamus. Gay biologist Simon Le Vay, well known for his paper on the differences in the hypothalamic structures between homosexual and hetero-sexual men, states in *The Sexual Brain* (1993):

In spite of the lack of such markers, the very existence of transsexuality speaks strongly, in my view, for the notion that gender identity is not necessarily determined by life experiences. For most 'core' transsexuals there simply is no history of traumatising experience, relationships, or illnesses that could possibly explain such a radical departure from conventionality. And transsexuals do not appear to be mentally ill ... I feel confident that biological markers for trans-sexuality will eventually be identified.

In early 1995 the Dutch researchers Swaab and Hofman, studying the brains of five MTF transsexuals who had died with Aids, found evidence of female structural development in the hypothalamus which confirmed results of earlier experiments on rats (Swaab and Hofman, 'Sexual Differentiation of the Human Hypothalamus in Relation to Gender and Sexual Orientation').

Empowerment by self-definition

When I went into the Gender Dysphoria Trust International office for my first counselling appointment I noticed a poster that said 'I am not a transsexual, I am transsexual'. A very simple statement, but what occurred for me was a subtle shift from feeling like a freakish object to recognising transsexuality as a human phenomenon and identity, followed by the realisation that being gender atypical and part of a small marginalised community does not mean transgendered people should be denied their humanity. The fact that there was a community at all made it possible for me to begin the transition. Its diversity and inclusiveness, embracing MTF/FTM transsexuals, transgenderists, transvestites, cross-dressers, third sex, intersex, non-labelled, drag queens, drag kings, gender-challenged, gender-gifted, shapeshifters, etc., came as a relief. You didn't have to contort your identity to fit into yet another narrow and oppressive category.

When people refuse to believe your account of your own gender experience your sense of authenticity and sanity is badly shaken time and again. It is no wonder that transgendered people internalise the shame, blame and the fear and hatred of others disturbed by what they experience as threatening and transgressive.

The struggle has been the right to self-naming and expression of identity, which has shifted in the community to questions about the necessity of passing for typically gendered people. Of course people's experiences vary, and many find their sense of gender identity approximates closely to one of the two accepted genders in the binary system. But for others, the experience of crossed or transposed gender is a strong part of their gender identity; being out of the closet is part of that expression. It is not really a debate about privacy and personal safety versus politics, so much as an impulse towards pride and a rejection of internalised transphobia. Some people choose to come out of the closet because doing so will help to educate the general public about the diversity and humanity of transgendered people and so ameliorate oppression in the future. I hope this book will be a contribution to the process of education and transgender pride.

New genders and pansexualities

❛ "Nobody fucking asks your date to show his dick, do they mouse? It's his own private business ... But, oh, no. They ask me. Tory's brother, that fuckface. What right does he have to ask me about my dick?" "He wants you to show him your penis? ... What are you going to do?" It did seem unfair that Paulie needed a penis to be a man. John Wayne would still be John Wayne if he had a vagina, wouldn't he? I didn't say anything like this to Paulie, but I hated Canon Quinn and Tory's brother, Rick, for not letting her see Tory. It wasn't as if Paulie were doing anything wrong, exactly. If the world didn't give boys so many advantages, Paulie wouldn't want to be one. At least, that's how I saw it then. Paulie saw it differently, because as far as she was concerned, she was a boy, period. ❜ Susan Swan, The Wives of Bath

❛ "Can you orgasm with that vagina?" — Audience member question to Kate on the Geraldo Rivera Show. "Yah, the plumbing works and so does the electricity." — Kate's answer. ❜ Kate Bornstein, Gender Outlaw

Transgender subjectivity

One of the questions most frequently asked of transsexual people is 'why do you think you are not the same gender as your anatomical sex?' Do these dysphoric people choose their gender any more than lesbians choose their sexuality? Do they convince themselves that their bodies are not the right ones for them, any more than lesbians convince themselves that they are not het-erosexuals?

A clue to this can be found in distinguishing between gender and sex, whose alignment is cultural rather than natural, and viewing the nature of identity as process. Gender can be divided into assignment, roles, identity, status, relational styles, attribution and biology, for example. They are all components but need not be consistent with each other.

Assignment, for instance, is the pronouncement of an individual's mor-phological sex based on a glance by a doctor at the time of birth, forming the basis of subsequent registration of gender status. Gender roles represent the expression of gender signals through appearance, dress, performance of gender behaviour and expected social tasks, such as jobs. Gender-role styles indicate masculine, feminine, androgynous or ambiguous. Gender identity is the subjective sense of being a gender, the sense of who I am. It is also the sense of belonging to one of the gender categories, or sense of what I am. This is a pivotal point for transgendered people, in that their sense of identity can be destabilised as it meets the gender attributions that others give them. If bodies and identities are separate things, then the reality of one's own experience of belonging to a category can easily be different from that of an attributor, especially if the observer believes in the coherence of sex and gender as a total system.

Everything that you live your life by, the values that you hold, these are all theories. They don't feel like theories because they're part of the dominant discourse, they feel normal. But in fact they are specific sets of assertions, about what bodies and sex and so on means. I'm just expressing and looking at it a different way. There are people who believe in male and female. That's a theory. It just doesn't feel like a theory, it feels like an essential truth. Riki Ann Wilchins

Both for the individual and for society, the dimorphic view of the human sexes (only two distinct anatomical forms) and gender is reinforced by medical, scientific and legal discourses and social discourses such as heterosexual family values. These say that you can only have one sex, which is assigned to you by medical professionals, and that your gender identity and role should correspond exactly and unproblematically to this 'fact' of sex, as should your sexuality, making you preferably heterosexual. Transgender says sex and gender ambiguity exists, that all identity is not coherent, that gender identity does not necessarily correspond to the genitals you have, that gender identity and sexuality are constantly fluid and in process.

The answer from transsexuals themselves about mismatches between gender status, gender identity and gender role and how they know that their identities are different from their bodies is usually: 'I just know; I have always known from earliest childhood.' This claim is not very convincing to most non-transsexuals. But these gender-gifted children, more changelings perhaps than ordinary tomboys and sissy boys, seem to know something that most of the adults in their lives will never know – that you don't have to play by the rules of gender. And with one magic wish or an eternal promise, they release themselves from those rules for ever more.

It's just something that I can feel. I wasn't aware of it until I had the surgery. I knew that I didn't want breasts. I wanted to get rid of them. And it took me a long time but I finally did get rid of them and after that I felt that I had to have a hysterectomy. I knew what I wanted to do but I didn't know why. And at the same time I always felt mentally androgynous. And then once I'd had the surgery and I had the body that I wanted and I felt that I was physically androgynous, I was able to discover and accept my identity. It's like my physical and mental selves had come together. Christie Elan-Cane

I had a recurring fantasy before I even realised I was TS (transsexual). I was walking down the street and I would imagine myself asking someone the time and that I would relate to them and they would see me as a man. Then I became aware of this embarrassing thought and I'd stop thinking it. But that's rather important, my interactions with people and them seeing me as a man. Not that I felt that there was something disgusting about my body or anything like that. Which I think for some TSs is the first thing they think. Martin

The overwhelming sense is that it is something not in the mind, but in the body or the brain. Brain-sex it is called. For some it is more ethereal, located in the soul. For others it is viscerally physical, of the soma, in the form of phantom penises, vaginas and breasts or the ablation of them. Or at one time or another for each person it is all of these.

[T]hat my conundrum might simply be a matter of penis or vagina, testicle or womb, seems to me still a contradiction in terms, for it concerned not my apparatus, but my self ... To me gender is not physical at all, but is altogether insubstantial ... It is the soul perhaps ... It is essentialness of oneself, the psyche, the fragment of unity. Jan Morris, *Conundrum.*

The female-to-male experiences a male body every single day of her life. Through strong engulfing fantasy, she 'feels' her broad shoulders, 'feels' her flat chest, her low voice. She feels a need to carry more bulk between her legs, and may wear padding. With this self-image, she is met in the mirror every single day of her life by someone she doesn't recognize. She knows she has a female body, but it is something that doesn't fit her self-perception. She knows she has breasts, but considers them growths that have no pleasurable sensation, and therefore wraps her chest and binds it flat so that her body conforms with this male self-image. Louis Sullivan, *From Female to Male*

Transgender narratives

[O]ne cannot take at face value transsexuals' own accounts of a fixed and unchanging (albeit sex-crossed) gender identity, given the immense pressure on them to produce the kinds of life histories that will get them what they want from the medico-psychiatric establishment. To take the problem one step further, the project of autobiographical reconstruction in which transsexuals are engaged, although more focused and motivated from the one that all of us pursue, is not entirely different in kind. We must all repress information that creates problems for culturally canonical narratives of identity and the self, and consistency in gender attribution is very much a part of this. Judith Shapiro, 'Transsexualism'

I went to the Gender Identity Clinic. They ask you questions you don't want to think about, that most people never have to think about. Things you always accepted are suddenly questioned. Questions like

'What makes you think you're male?' I mean, how many men can answer that? What makes you male? It's more than just the way your body is made. Suddenly you have all these questions to answer and they definitely affect the way you see yourself. Gerry

Narratives of transition, like coming out stories for lesbians and gays, are heroic processes of self-discovery and self-naming, from epiphany to acceptance, decision and commitment to change over, the embodiment or rebirth, the early stages of the new life and passing. It is during this process that some form of gender stability is sought, along with an alleviation of the anxiety and malaise of gender dysphoria. The form gender identity and role finally take can be more or less fixed or fluid, depending on the individual.

The chaos and often fear and pain of this lived experience become encapsulated into convenient narratives about the origins and realisation of the condition, through to arrival at the reassigned gender and the goal of one's new achieved sex through genital conversion. In fact because of the perceived radical undertaking of SRS, during their transition TSs must tell a multitude of stories to family, friends and employers as well as to themselves, doctors and psychiatrists in order to establish the 'truth' of the situation and allow evaluation of the sane and ethical deliberation which brought them to their decision.

With this comes the well-researched and rehearsed script or classic case history presented to the gatekeepers at the clinics in order to obtain successful treatment. Knowing that deviation from the script could jeopardise treatment, reproduction of the standard story supersedes truth. The gender clinics reinforce conventional, conservative, stereotypical gender behaviour and notions of an unambiguous, fixed and coherent gender identity, although the experience of most transgendered people is that identity actually evolves and changes.

I told them I am bisexual, but I prefer women. At the time that's how I viewed myself. I don't think that that was particularly the best thing to say. I thought, 'Why in hell should I lie and present all the classic case history that I'm supposed to present?' I tried to be as honest as I could. Which probably wasn't the best policy. So it took a long time. I felt that I lost five years of my life. A half life for five years. Caroline

I feel that the medical profession is full of crap. I had an argument with a psychiatrist two or three weeks ago about the fact that not all women are hetties and a lot of women don't want to be. Not actually telling her what I was thinking of being, but that might have been a threat to my treatment just telling her that. They should know that but it's a profession run by white middle-class hetties. And I find that very, very difficult. They're not in touch with the real world, some of them. They think that their way is the only way. Josephine Asher

Lou Sullivan was the first FTM to say to the authorities, 'I'm a gay man.' It wouldn't have been possible in Manchester or London then. And it's only just becoming possible now in the sense that people in the

community actually go out and educate people at Charing Cross [clinic] and say 'Do you realise people will identify as gay men and bi-sexual men?' They're only just beginning to get this message. Steven Whittle

Louis Sullivan, an FTM who died with Aids in 1991, came out to the gender community in the US as a gay man in 1989. Sullivan contacted Ira Pauly, one of the acknowledged pioneering researchers of transsexual psychiatry, in the hope of educating the professionals about the difference between gender and sexual orientation. Sullivan had been rejected by several gender clinics because he presented as a gay man.

One of the most insidious narrative forms required by the gender clinics, which is unique to the treatment for gender dysphoria, is the construction of a plausible, new personal history: a fictive account of childhood and life before transition, rewritten in the new gender.

Gender conflict is given embodied expression through surgery, producing the body as story. This transsexual body inscribed through 'textual violence' finally allows the representation of the contradictions and ambiguity, 'the chaos of lived gendered experience', to be intelligibly read (Sandy Stone, 'The Empire Strikes Back').

The only artform that's ever been afforded to transsexuals and trans-gendered people is the art of the autobiography. It's not a biographical statement, it's about subjectivity and the nature of being subjective. I think that this provides an immense wealth of information about how individuals can reconstruct, not just deconstruct notions of gender. Steven Whittle

I don't believe in male and female any more than I believe in transsexual. It is not possible to understand my body in those categories. I may in fact be a transsexual woman. We can argue about whether I'm female or not. We could also argue about whether I'm male. My body doesn't make sense within those terms. We enter into a process of cultural inscription that makes gender meaningful and intelligible. But it's not found in nature, it's found in language. Riki Ann Wilchins

Transition

The transition from living primarily in one gender role to another is fraught with difficulties. Some family members and friends who might prefer to ignore change, which may require them to change themselves, simply deny that anything is happening at all.

The first practical hurdle for people who know the person in transition is remembering the name and pronoun change. Some people refuse to change the pronoun even when it is obvious that they should. This is usually a source of major conflict, as it often means the non-transgendered person has not accepted the role change. Gender reassignment is distressing and difficult to understand for many non-transgendered people, who have not had their whole lives to get used to the idea, as the transgendered person has, and because it shakes up the primal belief in the permanence of sex and gender.

Marjorie Garber in *Vested Interests* refers to this 'pronominal confusion (pronominal dysphoria)' as 'an indicator of the boundary-crossing that makes gendered subjectivity so problematic'. Also gender is such a habit. It is critical to the way we treat other people and the way we behave, but the mechanism remains largely unconscious until someone transgresses, which sends immediate shock waves that something dangerous and unnatural is happening.

For the transgendered person living fulltime in the new role at the beginning of transition, presentation is ambiguous, sending out contradictory gender signals, so at each encounter it is usually impossible to guess how one is being perceived, whether they've got the gender right or in fact cannot make out what the gender is at all. This not knowing can cause hostility. Or people just stare. And they stare with impunity, as though the transgendered person was not a person at all.

There is always a gap between the moment transgendered people accept the truth about their gender identity and the point when everyone else perceives them in that identity. It often takes years. During that time the transgendered person is waiting for confirmation from bodily changes too. This also takes years to complete. When fully dressed one may have all that is necessary to be perceived socially in the right role, but there are schizophrenic moments when you catch a glimpse of your body in the mirror. Yet when gradually the changes do happen, there is euphoria.

There is also the 'urinary segregation' (Garber) enforced in public toilets. The inflexible either/or directly posits binary gender division, crossing of which is taboo. When the transgendered person in transition begins to use the other toilet, the breaking of this taboo and sense of transgression can cause anxiety. It is the fear of discovery but also, sometimes, the genuine confusion and inability to decide which is the correct one to use in one's between gender condition. Some people have to make alienating compromises in situations like work.

When the fuzzy line between social gender roles is crossed and the transgendered person in transition is perceived in the preferred role 98 per cent of the time, for some people that is the point transition has occurred. For others it is the actual embodiment after surgery which marks the end of the process. Before that, however, is the need to decondition and reconstruct oneself, get used to the gender specific expectations of others, like male bonding and unwanted sexual attention, and adjust to the gains, losses and new privileges that the transition brings and the unique experience being transgendered gives a person in such a rigidly gendered society.

Unfortunately, the better I passed, the worse I got along with women. Social interactions took on a me Tarzan/you Jane quality which the women themselves instigated. I knew I was the same me I had always been, but suddenly women were making demands that I not just talk, but also flirt, protect, know how to fix assorted mechanical gadgets, and lift pianos. If we were at their house, they would sometimes even hand me the keys and expect me to open their door. Kevin Horwitz, 'The Art of Passing'

I noticed I didn't have much remaining male privilege by the slow dawning of peacefulness in my life. That may sound flaky, but the fact is I'm nowhere near as territorial and possessive as I used to be. I'm not as frantic to get or hold on to something as I once was. I still want things. I still go after things. But I use force infrequently now. For me, that's a perk of having gotten rid of male privilege. The shortcomings are obvious: lower pay, less security, more fear on the streets, less opportunity in the job market. All those drawbacks made me look at the value of what I'd lost. Do I really want to take part in a culture that places a higher value on greed and acquisition than on peace and shared growth? Kate Bornstein, *Gender Outlaw*

When the subject of male privilege comes up, I usually laugh. I had more privilege as a female than I do now. But that's just a statement about the male pecking order (on which I am close to the bottom). I must admit that there is some male privilege ... for instance, I get a quicker, more polite response whenever I make business calls on the telephone; I feel safer on the street ... It's also easier to take a leadership role, because people take me more seriously. Overall, male privilege seems intangible – something that you can't quite put your finger on. Men pay a high price for these privileges, and I think that trans-sexual men pay an even higher price. Kevin Horwitz, 'The Art of Passing'

This is where I want to be, but it's not as though you don't pay a price. I had to give something up and there were hard things about that. You have to say good-bye to being a dyke. If I go to a lesbian gathering, basically nobody sees me. I'm invisible. Unless they know me and even then it's different. Women don't trust me as much. Max Wolf, unpublished interview with Cherry Smyth

Functioning genitalia

I think biology and genitalia in specific has a death grip on the culture's notion of gender. And I think it's going to be a long time before that melts away. And I think during that time, which I foresee as a long, long time, there are always going to be people for whom genital conversion surgery is necessary for their level of comfort. Kate Bornstein

As long as the naked body elicits responses from men and women, there will be transsexuals. Women who adjust their bodies to look like men do so to relate to men the way men relate to men, and to women, the way men relate to women, be they gay or straight. Louis Sullivan, *From Female to Man*

'He's agreed to show you.' Hebee was waiting, with his fingers splitting his pajamas, showing me his cunt, which was wide and lovely with folds and folds of pink skin. From inside came the limp cock and tiny balls too. I asked, 'Does

any of it work ?' … he said, 'It all depends on what you mean.' Darcy Steinke,
Suicide Blonde

The genitals and sexual practices of transgendered people are often material
for the horror, titillation and fascination of the media and non-transgendered
people. No matter how much transsexuals insist 'I am not my genitals', or
their partners acknowledge 'we make love to people, not organs', both TSs
and non-transgendered people are faced with the imperative of the existence
of 'cultural genitalia', despite what biological or achieved sexual anatomy a
person may have.

   In society people assume you have and attribute to you genitals which
correspond to your gender role presentation. This assumption allows intersex
people, pre-operative transsexuals and non-operative transgender people to
carry on social relations without threatening the traditional gender categories.
The destabilisation of gender categories is a transgression of boundaries which
violates profound taboos and causes horror, panic, repulsion, disorientation
and at worse a kind of existential schizophrenia. The pressure to keep fixed
and intelligible gender categories also creates anxiety for the gender intermediate person, who may seek to alleviate dissonance and anchor identity
by realigning it with sex, even after having claimed a dislocation between
biological sex and gender in the first instance.

**The most impressive thing about the hormones was growing a penis. I
thought that was definitely very worthwhile. That's something nobody
bothered to tell me about. I want the phalloplasty because I want to
be able to go swimming. I don't have a problem once I'm wearing my
swimming costume or when I'm dressed. It's the transition period
when you wonder if anyone is going to wonder …**

**I think if you have sex with me you need to know that I'm not built the
way you expect. I need to tell people before or it's not fair, and also I
don't feel happy about showing my body unless I know it's going to be
received well. But apart from that it's no one's business. What I feel I'm
telling people is: 'By the way I don't have testicles.' Some men don't
have testicles because they've had them surgically removed or
whatever; there are lots of ways of not having them. There are men
who for some reason have lost their penis or were born without; they
don't run around telling people. Why should I? And I don't think
there's any more to it than that.** Gerry

Other transgendered people for whom gender identity is not fully congruent
with physical genitalia, negotiate dissonance and expect gender to be destabilised within their own sense of identity and in society, but to the medical
and psychological establishment, whose task it is to maintain cultural norms
and stereotypes and not produce queers, this expression of diversity is invisible.

   While the genitals are not aligned with identity, celibacy is expected.
Transsexuals should be repelled by and unable to get pleasure from their genitals
of birth. So there is a silence around gender inappropriate sexual activity.

Learning the script for the gender identity clinics from the case studies in Harry Benjamin's textbook on transsexualism, the absence of reference to sexuality and an erotic sense of the body perpetuates a myth of low sex drive and sexual dysfunction.

I went and saw psychiatrists a couple of times. They gave me conflicting judgements. I'd slept with a couple of guys and quite liked it. At least one psychiatrist said, 'If you've enjoyed sex at all that means you're not transsexual. Because you'd be absolutely horrified at the idea of actually doing anything with your body.' So I was just completely confused ... In the late 60s that was the common attitude. Many of my older transsexual friends had been told that and therefore had to believe it in order to get through psychiatric counselling, and then experienced sex as a colossal problem, even when the surgery worked. People were encouraged to have unrealistic expectations. It's one of those stupid areas where doctors mess people about by just being ridiculously arrogant. Roz Kaveney

Determining which genitals are okay to have pleasure with, as sanctioned by the medical-psychiatric establishment, proves to be oppressive for TSs. Restrictive rules about what is gender appropriate sexual activity only encourage shame and guilt. It is considered clearly less pathological for transsexuals to have a fixation on having the right genitals than if they were to insist that they were women with penises or men with vaginas (Kessler and McKenna, *Gender*)

I like vaginal penetration. I like being fucked. I am not going to disown a part of my body which happens to be pleasurable for me. I would love to have a penis, but given the current technology right now that's not in the near future and what I have feels good and I want to use it. I found out from the person I see for counselling that she has a lot of FTM clients who like vaginal penetration. The thing is that nobody talks about it. David Harrison

If the medical-psychiatric establishment, through the gender clinics, cannot get transgendered people to conform to culturally sanctioned genital configurations and behaviour, to correspond to their social gender roles, then the legal system, backing up the medical establishment, will play its part in reinforcing the status quo.

The Human Rights Commission in the States is considering excluding transgendered people from the legislation that's being proposed – excluding gender orientation, only including sexual orientation.

If you look at legislation and proposed legislation for legal rights worldwide an awful lot of it includes surgical requirements, say for phalloplasty. So most of the FTM community can never access those legal rights or they go butcher themselves. It's appalling. Also nearly

all the legislation worldwide has a requirement of sterility before you can get your legal rights.

Are we really so far out, so inhuman that we have no right to reproduce? That we have no right for legal protection? My knowledge of the transgender/transsexual community is that they're the most human people I've ever met. They're the most sane and most ordinary people, in their madness, that I've ever met. Steven Whittle

Some TSs may feel a compunction to have functioning genitals which match their sense of gender identity, though they may still retain a critical position that their genitals do not need to be copies of typical genitals but are instead unique to the TS experience. For example, metoidioplasty is a genitoplasty which frees the clitoral penis of the FTM. This produces an intermediary type genital configuration, more like the penis of some intersex people. To want such genitals is to want the genitals of a TS man and not those of a genetic man. What is offered by the surgeons as a compromise instead of a fully functioning penis becomes for some FTMs an instance of transgender pride and a refusal of scarring and intrusive surgery which may destroy the potential of ever having an orgasm again.

Transgender community, culture, politics

Transgendered people have been accused of making an individual choice instead of a collective, political one in the struggle against gender role oppression and of being completely apolitical or – worse – reactionary, because of reproducing gender stereotypes and passing. But applying the lessons learned from early feminism that the personal is political, with 'consciousness raising' around shared experiences and oppression, a process of politicisation began in some of the support networks and in the alternative therapeutic/social groups during the 1980s. By the 1990s the Transgender Liberation Movement was born.

One of the reasons why so few transgendered people I know are political is because it gets knocked out of people. Someone I know was involved with an art centre that she'd helped set up – this was in the very early 1980s. She was a photographer and during a Reclaim the Night march had actually been responsible for several people's acquittal by producing advantageous photographic blow-ups of arresting officers which proved they were lying. And then the shit came down about her being TS and she was excluded from this art centre that she'd helped set up by women she'd kept out of gaol and they then did their best to lose her her job, 'cause she was working on *Gay News*. A number of women's groups told *Gay News* that they'd withdraw from listings unless she was fired. And she was, effectively; she resigned rather than be fired. It's the sheer inhumanity of that. That makes me very, very concerned about people's priorities.

One of the things that amazes me is how people who have been around politics for the last two decades have the nerve to complain that most transgendered people are apolitical. When they must know what was done to us and how we were excluded and how we still are. When did OutRage last mention transgender people? When did Stonewall ever mention transgender people? Roz Kaveney

F2M is a small network in New York which has existed for some time. An awful lot of the American local groups are created by therapists who are gatekeepers to services. They needed to provide a cost-effective but cheap form of therapy for their clients. They knew that personal one-to-one therapy is very expensive for their clients and for a lot of them it's inaccessible while they're trying to save up money for surgery. So what they do is try to provide an alternative by providing a therapeutic group system. It started out as group therapy and then it becomes a socialising, politicising thing. Steven Whittle

The major issues and campaigns of the transgender movement are: employment protection; being sent to the wrong sex prison; being unable to marry or adopt children; access to health care; legal status and changes of documents; action against transphobia and violence; action against defamation, discrimination and disinformation in the media; campaigning for inclusion in mainstream lesbian, gay and bisexual political agendas and human rights agendas; and, radically, working for the freeing of identity and the dismantling of the oppressive gender system.

At the beginning of the 1970s, in the early Gay Liberation Front years, there was a brief window concerning transgender issues, but by 1973–4, the orthodoxy hardened. Gay and radical feminist movements succeeded in suppressing and marginalising issues such as TS and cross-dressing. The question of inclusion came up again in 1985 during the public debates, confrontations and mass votes at the London Lesbian and Gay Centre concerning bisexuals, sadomasochists and transsexuals. Organisations such as Sexual Fringe made propaganda for the libertarian side of the debate.

Liberty, the National Council for Civil Liberties, has done work on transsexual issues since the 1970s, for example putting pressure on the Home Office to allow people to receive hormone treatment while serving prison sentences. Liberty's forthcoming Charter of Civil Liberties and Equal Rights Bill recognises the rights of TS people. Press For Change, affiliated to Liberty, is drafting a Policy on Transsexual Rights for Liberty to adopt and champion at a national parliamentary level. Liberty is also to bring a group action on behalf of Press For Change to the European Court.

Other British groups include the UK FTM Network, set up in 1990, which currently has 350 members and works to ensure that information on the social, health and legal needs of FTMs is made available.

In the US, lobbies and organisations like the International Foundation for Gender Education (IFGE), the American Educational Gender Information

Service (AEGIS) and the International Conference on Transgender Law and Employment Policy (ICTLEP) bring together trans-activists to fight for the civil rights of the gender community and promote awareness and acceptance of gender diversity. One relatively new group is Transsexual Menace, which in its first year campaigned on issues ranging from inclusion at Stonewall 25 to educating women going to the Michigan Womyn's Music Festival; as well as protesting at the Brandon Teena murder trials; developing dialogues with the Human Rights Campaign and the National Gay and Lesbian Task Force; working with the National Organization of Women on health provision; and collaborating with the Lesbian and Gay Anti-Violence Project on questionnaires to survey the violence experienced by TG people.

I think that the trans-liberation movement is going to really force the re-examination of the relationship between sex and gender expression and desire and also, if the movement is broad and inclusive enough, to show what a spectrum of sex, of gender expression, actually exists. The partitioning of the sexes, the legal edicts about how one can express self through gender expression, were a result of the division of society and class and no one movement alone can ultimately knock down those underpinnings of class society. It would take the unity of all people who are oppressed in this society to ultimately change it. I feel that trans-liberation is intrinsically tied to human liberation. I'm always hesitant to use terms about either sex or gender oppression that directly make analogies with racial and other oppression, because it's not the same struggle or the same fight, but it is against a common enemy. In order to have a really forceful struggle to bring about meaningful change, we have to forge coalitions. Leslie Feinberg

Gay and lesbian liberation originally started out saying: 'We are all queer. All people are queer.' They started out fighting for a radical freeing of identity and sexuality. And at the precise moment that gay liberation changed its rallying cry to 'Gay is as good as straight' it lost its moral focus and it lost its compelling message. Audre Lorde taught us that the master's tools will never dismantle the master's house. But it seems increasingly that the lesbian and gay liberation movement is no longer interested in dismant-ling the master's house, only in constructing a small, tastefully furnished addition at the back. Riki Ann Wilchins

As local or national groups and campaigns met and communicated via news-letters, a sense of community began to emerge. A realisation of numbers was especially brought home with the proliferation of transgender bulletin boards on the Internet, the global proportions of which have had a strong impact.

Where there is a community happening is online. There's a Transgender Community Forum, which has a huge mailing list. People who are very isolated get to talk about things with people who are

more in the thick of things. I think that sharing of information and ideas is where the revolution is happening. David Harrison

In Japan, there's a new FTM group just started. There's a group in Australia, a group in New Zealand. What will be really interesting is when we start to see the Eastern European countries and the Asian countries joining in. Steven Whittle

In the 1990s, alongside queer direct action groups such as Queer Nation and Lesbian Avengers, transgender direct action groups like Transgender Nation, Transsexual Menace and Transgender Rights, with local chapters throughout the US, were set up in direct response to the transphobia experienced by trans-people daily. Being out and proud versus passing has become the measure of the political consciousness and commitment of transgendered people, but the option of being out of the closet without serious repercussions in their lives is still not possible for many.

We talk about transphobia and gender phobia, so things have changed by virtue of the fact that we have language or words to discuss it. But otherwise, no, I don't feel that our oppression has changed. It's such an all-consuming and every minute of the day experience. Certainly transsexuals who pass and transsexuals who don't, face different experiences on the street. Those of us who are transgendered have a different set of experiences to people who are bi-gendered or to cross-dressers. But although we don't face identical oppressions, they really haven't been mitigated at all. We've just begun to really expose them in society, let alone to fight them, so I wouldn't even know how to begin to describe a day, except that it begins with people staring at me the moment I leave my house and it's punctuated with verbal and physical violence. Those of us who are transgendered really have to change society, because we're always going to be between, or in social contradiction to what people have been taught is natural. Leslie Feinberg

A tragic event which proved a spur to politicisation and the establishment of organisations to defend transgender human rights was the execution-style murder of FTM Brandon Teena and two of his friends in Humboldt, Nebraska in December 1993 and the subsequent distorted media coverage. As a consequence of his birth gender being exposed, Teena had been beaten up and raped a week before the murders, by the alleged murderers, one of whom was an ex-boyfriend of a woman Teena had been dating. When Teena reported the assault to the same police they did nothing, despite collecting over 100 pages of evidence and statements. Two men, who referred to Teena as 'it' and expressed no remorse, were each charged with three counts of first degree murder, and separate counts of rape, assault with a deadly weapon and kidnap. Although Brandon Teena's mother is quoted as saying Brandon never identified as a lesbian and hated being female, both the straight and the queer press referred to Teena as 'she' and as a 'cross-dressing lesbian' who, somehow, deserved what she got for her deceitful disguise. Many non-trans-gendered lesbians have also expressed their anger and outrage at Teena's murder and solidarity with TG people.

[L]esbians and gay men actually share the same stigma with 'transgendered' people: the stigma of crimes against gender ...

So let's reclaim the word 'transgendered' so as to be more inclusive ... Then, we have a group of people who break the rules, codes, and shackles of gender. Then we have a healthy-sized contingent! It's the transgendered who need to embrace the lesbians and gays, because it's the transgendered who are in fact the more inclusive category ... Only our bonding will permit a true revolution of sex and gender. Kate Bornstein, *Gender Outlaw*

The transgender community's need to see images of itself has led to a virtual Renaissance of art and literature. Trans-artists contribute to a broad-ranging and powerful re-visioning of trans-culture and identity.

In many ways the movement here is not new but the communities that make it up have been so deeply underground that many of the cultures and the humour, satire and creative forms have been underground and have been lost in mainstream society and even lost to other tributaries in the same movement. So we're just beginning to see a coalescing of these communities and sharing these aspects of pride. Leslie Feinberg

Class, race and other hierarchies

The cross-dressers get on with everybody. Transvestites, they're heterosexual, have a wife and kids, they tend to hate transsexuals. Certainly, in the Beaumont Society, there's a hell of a lot. I never met any other black TSs. I found that TV/TS club very, very destructive for me. And eventually I decided I wouldn't go back. Josephine Asher

As anywhere in society, the transgender community reflects race and class inequalities, but the microcosm also creates a hierarchy of its own between the categories of transgender. The hierarchy causes divisions between people along the lines of pre-operative and postoperative, FTM and MTF, but also class and race.

More inclusive memberships might be found in the working-class clubs. Jennie Livingston's documentary film *Paris is Burning* (1991), which portrays the Latino and African-American drag balls in Harlem, New York City, reveals a community which includes the spectrum of MTF transgendered people: pre-op TSs, transgenderists, she-males, drag queens and cross-dressers, cohabiting within their extended TG families. That isn't to say there wasn't some devision between family members.

It used to be that we were all gender trash rejects together. And when it became politically important, people who were postoperative started to be legitimated by the power structure that empowers non-transexuals and disempowers us. When we started to get empowered for having sex change surgery all of a sudden the distinction between post-op and pre-op became extremely important, as postoperative you got certain privileges and certain power.

Essentially surgery breaks down for me as a class and race issue. People who are economically empowered and want surgery, get it. Which means, essentially, people who are white and educated and largely middle class ... I also have a friend who's HIV positive. She can never get surgery. It's just too damn dangerous with the risk of infection and so on. So it also has to do with things like HIV and health. Riki Ann Wilchins

One of the expressed aims of the transgender liberation movement is to be truly inclusive and to unify the entire community around the common issue of gender and in defence of our human rights.

Because I'm lesbian it's much more logical for me, but I think there would be a lot of resistance to alliances from a lot of transsexuals because they identify as heterosexual women and don't want anything to do with the lesbian and gay community. Caroline

Outside the transgendered community, the various ethnic and religious communities from which trans-people of colour emerge either stigmatise or accept their TG behaviour in different ways from the mainstream culture. There is a link between race and gendered expression which informs the way gender is performed but also the way it is inscribed and represented in the fantasies and taboos of the dominant culture.

I was thinking about the whole notion of race, in particularly for this black FTM I know. Now, he's going to be seen as a black man, which has a particular resonance in Western society, because it's black men that people want to destroy and castrate. What is a black FTM's relationship to that? He's moving to a problematically privileged position. It's not like a white FTM who's now becoming top dog. How does the black FTM negotiate that, what kind of transition does that require? Inge Blackman

New labels and new vocabularies

Not only is social gender (that is, one's gender identity and social persona) independent of biological sex but so is one's sexual orientation identity, or SOID. According to sociologist Holly Devor in an article on the sexuality of FTM TSs ('Sexual Orientation Identities, Attractions, and Practices of Female-to-Male Transsexuals', 1993), SOIDS may be based on any or all of the following: 'genetic sex, morphological sex, sex identity, gender identity, gender role relational style, sexual fantasies, sexual desires, and sexual practices of oneself or one's partner(s) and/or the SOID of one's partner(s)'. Very importantly, these identities may change over the course of a lifetime and may be different with different people within a given time period. So an FTM TS, for example, could identify at various periods as straight, gay, lesbian, man or woman. The breaking down of sexuality into these component parts allows for potential recombinations, both erotic and non-erotic, the complexity of which remains largely unexplored in most relationships, although they may play a part in the fantasy life. Grimm in 'Toward a Theory of Gender' (1987) proposed a schema of 45 different possible combinations of two individuals in relationship to one another.

These terms throw some light on the subtleties involved in sexuality and desire and make it clearly obvious that the existing contemporary sexual identity classifications of lesbian, gay, bi and heterosexual, largely influenced by the work of Kinsey in the 1940s, are just the tip of the iceberg and are inadequate to describe the subjective experience of most people.

The term transhomosexuality was coined by Clare and Tully ('Transhomosexuality', 1989) to describe FTM transsexuals who became gay men. Stuart's 1991 study of 20 FTMs (*The Uninvited Dilemma*) seems to successfully debunk the myth that transsexuals are primarily homosexuals and lesbians in denial. Of her sample, 70 per cent had identified as lesbians before transition and 50 per cent had married men. Between 10 and 17 per cent identified as gay men after transition.

My research showed that of the FTMs that responded 33 per cent identified as bisexual, 40 per cent as heterosexual, 2 per cent as asexual and 25 per cent as gay men. So it's a much larger percentage than in the general population. In relation to MTF transsexuals, 50 per cent identified as lesbian women. It is laughable that MTF TSs represent stereotypes of women, when in fact the stereotype of woman they're representing is a butch dyke. Only 10 per cent identified as bisexual and 40 per cent as heterosexual. Steven Whittle

The first time I came across the term pansexuality was in an interview with David Harrison by Cherry Smyth for an article on transgendered lesbians and FTM TSs in *Attitude* (January 1995). The idea of pansexuality appealed to me and set my imagination to work. My own definition would be something like the following. With a heterosexual man I can be their best nightmare fantasy in the shape of a boy hustler. With a heterosexual woman I can be a pretty hetero male; or if I perceive her as a fag hag, I can be a faggot with bi tendencies. With a lesbian top femme I can be a high heel worshipping boy bottom or a third sex butch, a lesbian man. With a gay man I can be a cock worshipping catamite or a fisting top. With gender ambiguous bi men and women and sexually ambiguous transgendered people maybe I can just be myself.

Pansexuality, I think, is diversity. To me, it's an expression of orientation, meaning pan- as in panoramic, across lines. So it can mean that I
can be attracted to TS women, TS men, different kinds of men and
women. I like the word because it makes me think of Peter Pan or Pan
the love god. Now, I date men, mainly meeting them through personal
ads. I look for men who I describe as fluid in their sexual orientation. I
make that clear in my ads because a lot of straight men used to answer
them and they would expect a woman. And I'd say, 'I don't look like a
woman.' And they'd say, 'You have female genitals, right?' And I'd say,
'Yes, it would resemble female genitals.' And they didn't get it until
they actually saw me and then it didn't work, of course. It was not a
heterosexual dynamic. They were not accustomed to that. The men
I've had the most fun with are the men for whom their identity, their
orientation, is not an issue. Because inevitably if I'm with a straight
man and they enjoy having sex with me, at the back of their mind they
will think, 'Oh my God, maybe I'm gay.' Or if I have sex with a gay man
and they enjoy being with me, at the back of their mind, they're going
to go, 'Maybe I'm straight.' And so people I don't have to go through
that stuff with are either men who define as bisexual or who don't put
a label on themselves. David Harrison

What Devor calls the 'eclectic and voracious sexual tastes' of FTMs are usually
at least partly attributed to the increased libido which is a result of the testosterone. A percentage of MTFs who become involved in prostitution allow for
an exploration of fantasy and sexual practices which may be out of the
ordinary. TSs' involvement in non-genital based s/m play is also not surprising.
But perhaps what may be surprising, as transsexuals have been stereotyped
as either heterosexual or sexually neutered, is the configurations of relationships TSs find themselves in with both transgendered and non-transgendered
partners. Devor, looking at a sample of 45 FTMs, describes a 25-year relationship
of an FTM with a 'female, woman' partner which they both understood as a
gay man's relationship. As for MTFs, Anne Bolin's research contradicts the pro-
fessional literature which has heterosexuality intrinsic to transsexualism.

*Data from my research population on sexual orientation indicated far more
diversity in sexual preference than was commonly reported in the literature. Of
my sample, only one person was exclusively heterosexual, three of the six
exclusive lesbians were living with women who themselves were not self-
identified as lesbian, one bisexual was living with a self-identified lesbian, and
two male-to-female transsexuals were living with one another. This diversity
contradicts a paradigm that equates gender identity with sexual preference.*
Anne Bolin, 'Transcending and Transgendering'

It sort of came as quite a relief after I discovered my third gender
identity. I thought, 'I rejected men all those years ago, why should I be
interested in men?' The main reason that I'd rejected men was that
they perceived me to be a woman and yet the gay women who I'd

been with also perceived me to be a woman. And so looking at it a different way I thought, 'Well I'm just going to direct myself towards individuals who relate to me as an androgynous, third sex person.' It's how they see me, rather than how I see them really. And it's turned it around. The line between male and female just doesn't seem to exist any more. I've got my own partner now, who's an androgynous man. He lives as a man and he's happy with that, he wouldn't consider surgery. But he's not a stereotypical man. He has very much an androgynous mentality. He's very supportive of my identity. And he perceives me how I want to be perceived. Christie Elan-Cane

Danny requires that his partners recognize that he is a man before he has 'gay' sex with them ... though, he admits, there is room for the occasional misreading ... [H]e recalls that a trick he had picked up discovered that Danny did not have a penis. Danny allowed his partner to penetrate him vaginally because, 'it was what he had been looking for all his life only he hadn't realized it. When he saw me it was like "Wow. I want a man with a vagina."' Judith Halberstam, 'F2M'

In her book *The Apartheid of Sex: A Manifesto on the Freedom of Gender*, Martine Rothblatt suggests classification by colour as a new vocabulary for expressing sexual identity:

For analytic purposes, shades of color may provide a useful vocabulary for dissecting sexual identity. First, color comes in an infinite number of hues, allowing us to represent an infinite number of sexual identities. Second, the infinite hues can be grouped into chromatic categories. This permits a scientific classification of similar sexual identities. Third, colors can be combined to create blends.

Lesbians and transgender since the transsexual empire

❝ Despite theoretically embracing diversity, contemporary lesbian culture has a deep streak of xenophobia. When confronted with phenomena that do not neatly fit our categories, lesbians have been known to respond with hysteria, bigotry, and a desire to stamp out the offending messy realities ... [I]t is imperative to distinguish between emotions and principles. Just as "hard cases make bad law", intense emotions make bad policy. Over the years, lesbian groups have gone through periodic attempts to purge male-to-female transsexuals, sadomasochists, butch-femme lesbians, bisexuals, and even lesbians who are not separatists. FTMs are another witch-hunt waiting to happen. ❞ Gayle Rubin, 'Of Catamites and Kings'

❝ The question of deception must also be raised in the context of how transsexuals who claim to be lesbian-feminists obtained surgery in the first place. Since all transsexuals have to "pass" as feminine in order to qualify for surgery, so-called lesbian-feminist transsexuals either had to lie to the therapists and doctors, or they had a conversion experience after surgery. I am highly dubious of such conversions, and the other alternative, deception, raises serious problems, of course.

[Transsexuals] revert to masculinity (but not male body appearance) by becoming the man within the woman and ... within the women's community, getting back their maleness in a most insidious way by seducing the spirits and the sexuality of women who do not relate to men.

Because transsexuals have lost their physical "members" does not mean that they have lost their ability to penetrate women – women's mind, women's space, women's sexuality. Transsexuals merely cut off the most obvious means of invading women so that they seem non invasive. However, as Mary Daly has remarked in the case of the transsexually constructed lesbian-feminists their whole presence becomes a "member" invading women's presence and dividing us once more from each other. ❞ Janice Raymond, *The Transsexual Empire*

The transsexual Other: primal anxiety, frontier fears and taboo desires

Some lesbians have anxiety and fear about how easy it is to alter the body. Its mutability and the irreversible nature of the changes resulting from the hormones, even before any surgery, are terrifying when we have a sense of the entity of the body as certain and inviolable and fixed. Other major fears expressed by lesbians are to do with gender and sexuality categories blurring or breaking down, impacting upon their sense of lesbian community. What are transsexuals really? The effect on the identity of partners of TSs, the impact on butch identity, the alienness of the constructed genitals of MTFs all have resonances for lesbians. Resistance to dealing with one's own sense of fear, discomfort, ambivalence and prejudice, and feeling forced to change one's safe, familiar view of the world, also contribute to anxiety.

More transsexuals also now exist who do not pursue a complete change. Increasing numbers of individuals utilize some but not all of the available sex-change technology, resulting in 'intermediate' bodies, somewhere between female and male ... Some of these may not want to leave their lesbian communities, and they should not be forced to do so. They may cause confusion, repelling some lesbians and attracting others. But if community membership were based on universal desirability, no one would qualify ... Our society should be as inclusive, humane, and tolerant as we can make it. Gayle Rubin, 'Of Catamites and Kings'

Male-to-female transsexuals feed into that fear, in for example Jan Raymond's book, that scientists are going to create a race of perfect women. Alison Gregory

The question is what are these people going to be when they've changed sex? That is what threatens. When it's a lesbian becoming a man, what they really want to know is who are they going to sleep with? Are they going to sleep with straight men, gay men, straight women, lesbians? It's that bit that bothers them because in terms of lesbian identity, I think there's a huge identification issue. And where does this lesbian go ? Do we just lose them into the abyss out there because they change sex? Annette Kennerley

The FTM presence at Powersurge (the leather dyke conference in Seattle) last year made me uncomfortable. A lot of this is my personal garbage. I am afraid that the visibility of FTMs will change the definition of what's butch until women will feel they have to take male hormones to make them masculine enough to be butch. I am afraid other people will judge my own strategies for dealing with gender dysphoria ... [T]he leather dyke community is very competitive. Labels are important to us and we stigmatise women who don't meet our expectations of the roles we have assigned them ... I'm afraid of not qualifying, not counting, being second-rate. Being uncomfortable is not necessarily a bad thing. Any time I try to absorb some new information, I have to tolerate a period of ambivalence and ambiguity. Pat Califia, 'Who is my Sister?'

[O]ur mere presence is often enough to make people sick. Take that great scene in the film, The Crying Game *... The revelation of Dil's gender ambiguity called into question both the sexual orientation (desire) and the gender identity of Fergus. His vomiting can be seen as much as a sign of revulsion as an admission of attraction, and the consequential upheaval of his gender identity and sexual orientation ... heretofore unquestioned states of very personal identity.* Kate Bornstein, *Gender Outlaw*

I'd met a male-to-female transsexual. And that freaked me out and I thought, no I can't cope with this. In essence your body is still male, even with the operation. S. told me what the operation involved. And I guess if she hadn't told me that – that it is the penis and it's been inverted – then maybe I wouldn't have reacted the way I did. But my reaction was, 'Oh my God, that is a cock.' And I just didn't want to be anywhere near it. Kacha

Lesbian feminist politics

Feminists struggled to reclaim lesbianism from the oppressive designation of pathology created by nineteenth-century sexologists and its persistence as a listed mental disorder in the American Psychiatric Association's *Diagnostic and Statistical Manual* (till 1973). Feminists sought to purify the category of lesbian. A pure lesbianism was fashioned and boundaries drawn to determine who was to be included and who was not. The characteristic of sameness based on common experience of oppression due to the social status of women became conflated with biological/anatomical sameness, exacerbating the biological link to gender.

For cultural feminism the source of an authentic woman's consciousness had its roots in the female body as testament and 'truth'. Radical feminism mapped women's territory within those boundaries which grew out of that 'truth'. Revolutionary feminism, which pointed out that the system of patriarchy was upheld by the actions of individual men, meant that it became even more critical to be able to designate who was a man and who was a woman in order to distinguish oppressor from oppressed. The commonsense belief that it was self-evident what a man/woman was meant the categories themselves were not questioned.

Hiking Dykes, a walking group, split over the issue of whether a transsexual could join the group or not. The feminist argument against allowing transsexuals to be part of a woman only group was that they don't have a woman's past. They weren't brought up as women and because so much of the women's movement was premised on personal experience and sharing that experience and theorising out of that,

feminists argued for exclusion of transsexuals. The other reason is the practical experience of actually being in groups with transsexuals. It's probably unfair to judge all transsexuals on the ones that one has come across. But it's very difficult for people to lose the habits of their gender upbringing. Male-to-female transsexuals in women's groups dominate, in my experience. In this society women have little enough space and time for their voices to be heard. So if they form a group so that they can have women's voices heard they don't really want to have a man there. Rosemary Auchmuty

It was weird for me to sit in a room full of dykes and watch them listen respect-fully while FTMs talked about wanting to cut off their tits. But when the handful of MTFs who had come to the workshop dared to speak out, the hostility toward them was palpable. FTMs take male hormones so they can look as masculine as possible. They wear penile prostheses in their pants and cross-dress. Most of them would have surgery to give themselves penises if they could afford it and if the surgery could create a fully-functional male sex organ. Why do these folks qualify as 'leather dykes' when MTFs don't? MTFs take female hormones, love their tits, often undergo painful surgery to create female genitals, and live full-time as females and as dykes. It made absolutely no sense to me that FTMs were welcome at a [leather dyke conference] when MTFs were not.

I think MTF dykes have earned the right to be part of my community. Not every MTF is my close personal friend or somebody I'd want to sleep with, but they certainly are not the enemy. Pat Califia, 'Who is my Sister?'

Even socialist feminism, which looks at the material circumstances of oppression, assumes that 'natural' gender divisions are the basis of inequality and disem-powerment.

Neither gender is a bit of a difficult concept to crunch in a society which structures identity through gender. What does it mean? There would be an enormous shift in the mode of structuring identity. I don't know if the proliferation of gendered identities is deconstructive or not. I suspect it's no more or less deconstructive than if you just have gay people hanging around. I don't think it's going to make any amount of difference to the way the dominant figures. In terms of the strategy in relation to gender, transgendered people tend to fit more into a reactionary strategy than a radical strategy. A radical strategy wouldn't accept a biological argument for human domination and subordination. Paula Graham

Transgender is seen by feminists to be politically reactionary and an individual solution to what is a collective problem.

I don't see male-to-female and female-to-male transsexuals as equivalent in any way. I don't define male-to-female transsexuals who

become lesbians, as lesbians. I don't think they should be in women only spaces because I don't think they are women. A male-to-female will always be a man whether he's had his penis cut off and breasts put there or not. As far as I'm concerned, he is a man. Men are brought up with much more status than women. He hasn't been brought up with the same oppressions as women. I wouldn't trust him and I wouldn't want to have anything to do with him.

In terms of female-to-male transsexuals, it's different because, yes, they've been brought up as a woman but, no matter what individual reasons they feel there are for doing it, they become part of the class of oppressors. There are a lot of advantages to living that way. It's a complete fucking cop out. In a lot of ways it would be easier for us all to bloody live as men. They have got so many more privileges. To me it's an individual solution to the collective oppression of women. And that's why it enrages me because I don't think we can ever find solutions on an individual basis to a society that absolutely fucks women over. I am suspicious of those women because I think they are making alliances with men and taking privileges that men have but still wanting to be part of the support system that they get from women. In fact they want the best of both worlds. I would exclude those women from the lesbian community. Hilary McCollum

I think there's becoming less and less affirmation of women being attracted to women. It seems now that the only really sexy lesbian sexuality is one that's very phallocentric. What does that say about us as women, that we have to take on a masculine body to attract women? Inge Blackman

Feminism questioned the content of gender roles, demanding expansion of them and changing the balance, claiming that gender shouldn't matter any more and that it was a false constraint. Although, for some, lesbian is a separate gender category to woman, when political lines against patriarchy are drawn the binary is reinvoked. This may be necessary as a strategy but what are the consequences as a description of reality? The fact that some women, some lesbians, actually fell on the border or beyond as well as on either side of the line failed to provoke a dissolution of the categories altogether.

What is it that makes you want to go further into something much more to do with gender, not about being a lesbian or being butch? I think there's got to be another element, because you can be as butch as you like and why do you need to do anything more? But it's interesting that in a more liberal climate there are still butch lesbians who want to have a sex change. This is something more than lesbian politics can encompass and I think that's what is threatening people. Annette Kennerley

Separatists have re-entrenched behind the view of gender as bi-polar, policing the borders. Not only do multiple genders seem unthinkable in separatist lesbian feminism, they are simply not the issue. But at a time in our culture when gender is a burning issue, separatism seems an obsolete tool for making sense of the world. All difference, not just men, maleness and patriarchy, has become a target of suppression. Inevitably the unique and complex experiences of and the differences between lesbians can not be subsumed within the boundaries of the 'pure lesbian'.

I think lesbian separatist feminist politics has had its day now. Maybe it was necessary at the time. There's always a reason for separatism in any political movement, but ultimately you come back out of that. I think men have the potential to change. You've got to believe that really. The best way to do it is by contact and influence and being brought up as boys by people who are committed to that. And if women are becoming men, they'll make very different men than a lot of the ones around. Maybe that's the argument to reclaim male power. We've tried to get power and be equal to men in so many ways, why not have their bodies and experiences too? The ultimate way to take power off them is to create a new man. What better way to do it than out of our own bodies? Annette Kennerley

Robin Morgan is interesting because she actually precedes Daly in the argument that if a lesbian-identified transsexual sleeps with another lesbian woman and doesn't mention their sexuality, then it's rape. Because it's deceit. Roz Kaveney

First, class differences expressed in terms of female masculinity and butch/femme were duly excommunicated. Then race and ethnicity raised conflicts when black lesbian feminists refused to give up the common struggle against racism with the men in their communities, even if that meant criticising racist white feminists, making it very clear that all women are not the same. With no discussion, male-to-female transsexual lesbian feminists were vilified and expelled as infiltrators, followed by s/m, queers and now the new Other: female-to-male transsexuals and transgenderists. The latter are seen as tainted by mixing with gay men. Rad fems cite lesbians working with gay men around Clause 28 and Aids issues as the latest reason why lesbian feminism is losing the support of lesbians, not the expulsions or constraints with which they exclude most lesbians who don't tow their line.

I think the reason that transgender is coming into the lesbian community is because of our increased association with gay men. That partly came out of Clause 28, which was a turning point where lesbian feminism lost its support in the lesbian community.

I think female-to-males who identify as gay men are to do with the way gay male culture has become glorified within the lesbian community in the past ten years. And Cherry Smyth's kind of line, 'a chick with a dick', the playing on dildos and dicks and fucking gay men and getting into the whole body beautiful culture, that is gay men. It's something that's taken over the lesbian community in the past seven

or eight years. And so I don't think it's that surprising that lesbians are having sex changes to become gay men. Hilary McCollum

I find FTMs becoming gay men the most understandable element of it really, because you're not leaving a gay construct. But why you would go to all that trouble to remain within a gay construct, is slightly mysterious. I see it as having to do with the mystique of the phallus, which permits one to appropriate a male position without entering into relations of domination with women. It's a perfect solution in a way to the power imbalances. You can have your dick and eat it too. Paula Graham

Outside the separatist enclave of lesbian feminism, at the grassroots, other lesbians get on with their lives, bringing lesbian feminism to a maturity which reflects the real diversity among lesbians now, even if this does not add up to a coherent community.

I do think that [separatist feminists] are only a small group of women. I think they were always a small group of women. I think that they were just vocal. Queers do want the feminist label but I don't think we've been so interested in identifying as lesbians. They were trying to stake out a territory that was specifically lesbian and they did it very success-fully. And, now, if you're interested in women-identified-women, women-loving-women, you know where to go. Coffee-shops, bookstores, etc. I just hope that the gender community comes up with something that's a little more confrontational and not as separatist. Judith Halberstam

Like any other social group, transsexuals and other transgendered people exhibit the social and political range, from reactionary and conservative to progress-ive and radical. Some FTMs want male privilege and power and are sometimes overcompensatingly sexist in their treatment of women. Others want male bodies but feel that male stereotypes are oppressive for themselves and others and fight to deconstruct male privilege.

I think it's easy for me to challenge other men on sexism, being very out as gay. I'm almost expected to confront them on what's going on. Maybe if I was straight I would find it more difficult. Martin

I find there's no excuse for misogyny and I do hear it among FTMs. Sometimes it's those guys who haven't gone through lesbian feminism. But sometimes with the younger ones there's a lack of consciousness. I still think that trying to emulate what the culture considers to be male is a waste of an opportunity to go beyond that. David Harrison

Some MTFs do want to be the dependent bit of fluff draped over a man's arm and want to obey him and reinforce his power. Others are feminists and lesbians and don't want to have anything to do with men because they have been abused by men, individually or by the system of patriarchal power.

I suppose the worst part of my life was when I went through the period of going with men. I was naive and men exploited me, they just wanted to find out what their own sexuality was and they used me to do that. The reason I'm so angry with men is a hangover from that. I felt very used and exploited. Josephine Asher

Ironically, as a marginalised and disempowered group, transgendered people seem to have some inordinate power to uphold and maintain the gender system. This allows us to be blamed for gender: because we alert people to the fact that gender is not natural, gender somehow becomes the fault of transgendered people.

Trans-people become society's gender trash that it wants to sweep under the carpet and forget. Seeing the diversity of transgendered people and not just the stereotypes is how feminists, lesbians and gays, differently abled people and other oppressed or marginalised people will recognise trans-people as allies instead of opponents.

Transgender politics is raising the consciousness of transsexuals and other gender-challenged people, helping us to find pride and solidarity and so to heal the trauma of growing up transgendered in a culture that stigmatises and pathologises that experience. In this way the stereotypes and bi-polar gender itself are being challenged, the need to pass is being challenged, and the need to create lies about one's past and one's status as transgendered becomes less compelling and even counterproductive. But that also requires educating and challenging non-transgendered people around one.

I think that each movement gets to a new layer in deconstructing gender. Feminists thought they could do it. Bisexuals argued they could, lesbian and gay, then queer and now transgender ... If only they could be brought together and things would change. But I don't think history works like that. It's so much more haphazard and random.

Is Kate [Bornstein] a failed transsexual because she says I'm neither a man or a woman? Did it not work for her or is that what we're all going towards? She had to go through the surgery to come to that position. You can't say I can be neither from this point of view. You have to go through it. And that's what a lot of people find difficult. If you really believe in the possibility of being non-gendered, mult-igendered, then why change? That's where most feminists get lost in the argument. Cherry Smyth

But still for some TSs whose gender identity is completely transposed, the dissonance of identity and physical body is unbearable, aggravated by others attributing the wrong gender to them because their body presents something else. This means that some TSs will continue to need to change their bodies by surgery to approximate something closer to their sense of self. For other transsexuals and transgendered people, only partial modification with hormones is necessary and in milder cases of gender dysphoria cross-dressing might be sufficient.

Some people just want to explore, experiment or play with gender, pushing against the rigid categories, stereotypes and norms, blurring, bending and fucking with gender expectations. Very few people can cross-live, get employment successfully and be safe in the streets without hormones and some surgery. Many feminists see the choice of hormones and surgery as politically deluded because of risks to the individual's health and the dependency on a patriarchal medical establishment, but also because it is seen as collusion and has implications that other gender 'aberrant', rebellious people, especially children, could be forced to undergo similar treatment to bring them in line with the status quo. There is also a notion of the natural – of bodily integrity being tampered with and violated – and of colluding with consumer capitalism's misogynist body image fashions.

A feminist argument proposes that it's actually in the government's interest to provide these operations, because they would rather have people living the gender role they want to than have people who are one sex, but stretching the limits of that sex beyond what they would want. In other words, they would rather have transsexuals than lesbians and gays. They would rather have people fitting into heterosexual society. Rosemary Auchmuty

Surgery is seen as self-mutilation and the result of some form of deep self-hatred or hysteria. Rad fems in their arrogance believe they know best what's good for other people. They don't seem to listen or hear when transgendered people say they are healing themselves and choosing the best options to turn around dysfunctional lives, fully accepting the health risks of the surgery (which is radical and intrusive) and hormones (which increase the likelihood of breast cancer in MTFs and liver cancer in FTMs, among other conditions). It is worth the risks to live their lives as themselves and as they choose, not as someone else chooses for them.

Self-mutilation is the abusive action of someone who hates themselves. I don't deny that, and it engenders further self-dislike often by incurring the distaste of others. Gender reassignment surgery, on the other hand, is to change the body in ways that will enable the person to be more comfortable in themselves. Which in my opinion is completely the opposite. Gerry

The UNITY and Inclusion benefit for Camp Trans, a watershed event which may change the direction of lesbian feminism beyond the issue of transsexual inclusion, was held at the Lesbian and Gay Community Centre on 29 June 1994. The benefit was to raise funds to support a camp that would offer workshops on transgender to women attending the Michigan Womyn's Music Festival, which has a 'women-born-women' policy and excludes MTF TSs. Speakers and performers at the event included Amber Hollibaugh, Minnie Bruce Pratt, Holly Hughes, Kate Bornstein, Leslie Feinberg and Riki Ann Wilchins.

The lesbian feminists who spoke at the Camp Trans benefit, by reclaiming the fight against gender oppression as central to feminist activism, have claimed taking responsibility for construction of one's own identity and desire – which may mean by choosing to take sexual risks – as a feminist act. This runs counter to both the 'pure, safe haven' concept of women's community and to the concept of conformity to a collective standard instead of one's own conscience. It also reflects a new maturity on the part of lesbian feminists, a security in the strength of our woman-centered lives amidst a patriarchal society. Beth Elliott, 'AND? AND? AND?'

My argument is that a biological determinist policy is harmful and could set back the entire women's movement, theoretically affect it and skew its direction. But that a policy of 'all women welcome' is really going to revitalise the women's movement and I'm finding a very receptive ear. Leslie Feinberg

Is biology destiny?

One is not born, but becomes a woman. No biological, psychological, or economic fate determines the figure that the human female presents in society: it is civilization as a whole that produces this creature, intermediate between male and eunuch, which is described as feminine. Simone de Beauvoir, *The Second Sex*

In some cases, some transsexuals, some transgendered people do jump from one box into the other and are reinforcing the binary. But fewer and fewer true feminists who are really looking for gender freedom are buying that. They're listening to what transgendered people have to say and a lot of transgendered people these days are saying, 'No I'm not a man, no I'm not a woman. I'm something else under the sun.' And that is so much less threatening to feminists who are in fact struggling against the same binary we're struggling against. We are in fact this new wave of transgendered people, holding up the same 'biology is not destiny' button that feminists have been holding up for a long time. I agree with Sandy Stone and Riki Ann Wilchins when they say that this transgender movement is simply the next logical phase of feminism. Kate Bornstein

Lesbian feminists and transgendered people each accuse the other of taking a bio-determinist view of gender. Transsexuals in particular are seen to uphold society's gender status quo by changing their bodies to fit desired gender roles, as if they were having sex conversion surgery in direct response and as a solution to rigid gender roles and not because of their compelling experience of transposed gender identity. But radical lesbian feminism seems, to transgendered people, to invest in the same dominant discourse of dimorphic sex and binary gender as the hetero-patriarchy. Feminism may be in opposition to patriarchy, but it seems to accept the basic premise and agree to the terms of essentialised gender in creating its oppositional view.

I do tend to see transgender as reactionary in the sense that much of the discourse around it is biologist and it has a tendency to reinforce that notion that gender is biological. It fits in basically with the reactionary forces which are attempting to stem the flow of gender change. Paula Graham

It's almost like saying gender is fixed if I feel like a man trapped in a woman's body or a woman trapped inside a man's body. That I've got to change the external to fit the internal, not challenge the external. There are different types of women; some women can be hairy, have beards, can be aggressive. There are some men who can be passive, almost prototype feminine, but have an external masculine body. There's nothing really that actually challenges that so far, that I've seen. But at the same time, an FTM that I know has gone through radical changes; he's become more confident and become somehow more at peace with himself. Individually, people have turmoil that they feel can only be changed by surgery, and that is a personal journey, but I'm looking at it in a wider context and what that says about gender. Inge Blackman

The man trapped in a woman's body metaphor, and vice versa, inaccurately describes the experience of most transgendered people, yet it has become an easy one for the mainstream media to latch on to and it persists. It is a short-hand used by transgendered people when avoiding long discussions with a traditionally gendered person, especially if s/he is a bigot or basically not prepared to think about the issues. Many transgendered people feel they are not the gender they were assigned and are not comfortable with their birth sex; beyond that, they feel varying degrees of identification and belonging to another gender category. Most often gender is fluid and identity evolves. The achieved anatomy is a way of relieving the confusion and anxiety, and the body is a point of reference, not a nature.

Minnie Bruce-Pratt has written this book *S/He*. She talks about how she was brought up in the south and was made to see whiteness as natural and how that always seemed to her completely wrong and she got a real sense of injustice. And her position on that reminds her of her position around transgender, that she thought gender was natural. And she's had to completely reconstruct everything she thought. Cherry Smyth

When confronted with transsexuality, radical feminism reverses Simone de Beauvoir's 'anatomy is not destiny' insight, with claims that our gender reality and destiny are bound by chromosomes. This sets back the course of feminism, aligning it with the establishment it is critiquing.

Even chromosomal sex is not an absolute. There are occurrences which are neither XX or XY and, in conjunction with other factors like hormones, can yield unexpected anatomical combinations. Assignment would seem to be the site of determining power which fundamentally affects gender, rather than the invisible factors of biological sex. It is morphology that is the basis of that assignment. But when anatomical sex is altered because of errors in assignment or surgical conversion, the search by others for the true sex of those altered individuals reinforces biology over ideology.

Even XX chromosome women can fail the Barrbody test, used to test athletes, because the appropriate number of Barrbodies which need to be present to indicate femaleness, when counted under a microscope, is not consistent from one day to the next. What methods will lesbians use, in spaces that exclude all but XX chromosome women, to determine the gender status of women attending?

I used to be much more essentialist than I am now. I believed that men were genetically deficient and I believed that I was born butch. When I lived in Israel and I had to be in the closet I suddenly became much more social determinist. In my MA thesis, I tried to prove through the history of biology and physiology that biological sex is an absolute continuum. And it's a completely artificial divide. There's no medical way whatsoever of proving who is a man and who is a woman. Which is why they have all these problems at the Olympics. I wish that it was really no more significant than the colour of your eyes. I've never felt like it was anybody's business what my gender was. But you can't exist without a gender for political reasons and I always identify as a woman for that reason. Spike Pittsberg

There are, in addition to the XX and XY pairs, some other commonly-occurring sets of gender chromosomes, including XXY, XXX, YYY, XYY, and XO. Does this mean there are more than two genders?

Let's keep looking. What makes a man – testosterone? What makes a woman – estrogen? If so, you could buy your gender over the counter at any pharmacy. But we're taught that there are these things called 'male' and 'female' hormones; and that testosterone dominates the gender hormone balance in the males of any species. Not really – the female hyenas, for example, have naturally more testosterone than the males; the female clitoris resembles a very long penis – the females mount the males from the rear, and proceed to hump. While some female humans I know behave in much the same manner as the female hyena, the example demonstrates that the universal key to gender is not hormones. Kate Bornstein, *Gender Outlaw*

Transsexuals are usually certain about their subjective experience of gender, their gender identity. It is their anatomical sex, sex assignment and attribution by others that are in contradiction to that subjective sense of themselves. Gender could be said to be destiny for transsexuals (Judith Shapiro, 'Transsexualism'). The goal is corrected attribution of gender. It seems to be a liberation from what is, for most, the physical fate of what they were born with. This disconnection of identity, attribution, social role from anatomical sex as the foundation and 'natural' sex as the only reality of gender, puts gender up for grabs – what it is, who has it and in what form or combination, seem to make transgender the heir to the 'anatomy is not destiny' legacy.

What if transsexuality was found conclusively to have a biological basis?

I would say that if transsexualism was found to have a biological basis, that would be seen as maintaining heterosexuality, and that's a problem for lesbians and gays because it would put lesbians and gays more out on a limb as people who were resisting the need for men to be like this and women to be like this. We're actually saying that a man and a woman should have the chance to be like anything and then you wouldn't need to have surgery and that is the society I'd like to work towards. The other thing I would be worried about is that there would be pressure on gays and lesbians to have surgery as well. There would be some kind of argument that 'X and Y and Z were able to convert to being men, why don't you do that? And then we'll all be happier. If you want to wear trousers why don't you become a man?' Rosemary Auchmuty

Stone butch blues

In *Gender Trouble* Judith Butler quotes a femme lesbian who explains that she 'likes her boys to be girls'. What this means is that far from reproducing heterosexuality, the presence of masculine codes in a 'culturally intelligible "female body"' is what produces a transgressive tension which generates desire for the femme. The dissonant juxtaposition and interplay of female body and masculine identity destabilise both terms, displacing them from the heterosexual into the lesbian context with highly erotic consequences. In the way that the raw material of s/m is power, the raw material of butch/femme is gender.

Although butch tends to get a lot of attention in the discussion of gender trouble, femme too does not reproduce heterosexual femininity but displaces it within the context of lesbian desire, which denaturalises it by adopting a self-parodying critical distance and by being the object of the butch's desires. 'The category "femme" is not monolithic – it may not even be a sub category of "lesbian". They occupy a gray area that is matched … by the stone butch's own ambiguity' (Heather Findlay, 'Modern Stone').

Along what seems to be a butch continuum, you will find some pre-op and non-op FTM transsexuals who are only distinguishable from some stone butches in their identification as not-women, creating a grey zone. Although some butches do become FTMs, the distinction remains that between gender and sexual style. But as far as transgendered people are queer, they will share a common cultural space with queer lesbians.

I see butch and transgender as utterly separate things. I don't see any real connection, unless it's the visual, body style. Butch to me is a specifically lesbian identity and way of being and a social and political

statement, tied up with some kind of resistance. I don't think transgender is a lesbian thing. I think people can come from all kinds of places in the world and feel that they are in the wrong body. I don't think it's a lesbian construct. I think it's a gender construct. Spike Pittsberg

A stone butch is a lesbian who gives her femme lover pleasure but will not allow the femme to touch her sexually, penetrate or bring her to orgasm. Being stone butch has been characterised as aberrant or tragic as a result of internalised misogyny because she is not accepting of her female body.

For most stone butches it's just a way of indicating what kind of sex they like to have: everybody has limits to what they'll do and what they want done to them sexually. They question why having a certain anatomy should dictate the types of sexual pleasure you must have with that anatomy. Other stone butches are clearly gender or genital dysphoric. Stone butchness is an identity and strategy which work to a greater or lesser degree and may change over a lifetime.

Lesbian transgendered fantasies and desires

In so far as this new Other is taboo or dangerous, threatening one's own sense of gender and sexual identity, and thrilling because of the unknown, transgender is eroticised.

There's a whole body of work waiting to be done on who's attracted to gender ambiguous bodies. Why is it that, if I'm identifying as a stone butch, someone who uses very little of her femaleness, I do find partners? I've found there are lots of women out there who are very interested in both the non-mutuality of sex that you're going to have, where it's not I do you, you do me. That's one component of it, and the other is the contradiction between presenting male and being female. And that is a very specific desire. That's one we haven't looked at very much as lesbians. Because the lesbian community is so invested in coming up with egalitarian notions of sexual desire and sexual fluidity that we didn't properly account for the fact that some women were going to build entire sexual practices around non-mutuality, inegalitarianism and absolute difference. And that's butch/femme, s/m and every other non-vanilla sexual practice. Judith Halberstam

The sense of a single and coherent gender or sexuality identity is illusory. At the boundaries of the lesbian erotic, non-transgendered lesbians meet their own transgendered desires. As with butch/femme, the interplay or the juxtaposition of a lesbian identity with a not always culturally intelligible gendered body or a transgendered body produces an erotic tension in the destabilising of gender and identity terms, which generates complex and unpredictable dissonances and, potentially, an entire new spectrum of desire. '[G]ender dysphoria within lesbian circles is often embraced and channelled within sex play as a libidinal force' (Judith Halberstam, 'F2M').

Transgender fantasies disrupt rigid gender categories by proliferating identifications and multiplying gender positions. They deconstruct and send into orbit heterosexist structures as well as lesbian rad fem constraints. In lesbian sex clubs and sex 'zines, as in lesbian bedrooms or public sex venues, queer identities have been evolving from butch/femme to unabashedly transsexed play with its hermaphroditic, bisexual dissonances for the fantasiser.

I suppose a lot of my fantasies are in a sense bisexual and transgendered. I like the idea of being with someone who's got breasts and a cock. Who's got muscles and a vagina. Who likes getting fucked in the ass, who likes playing different parts. I don't often think of them being a male body with a vagina, but I've never had sex with a TS to my knowledge.

I have a fantasy life that is informed by transgender in a way that is much richer for me than butch, 'cause I couldn't act butch. I mean, I know I'm femme. It's so funny. I couldn't learn to be butch but I could become a man. That's really weird. It's like David [Harrison] was a femme dominatrix and now he's a man. Cherry Smyth

The 'daddy-boy' lesbians of the 1990s may be less concerned about becoming 'real lesbians' ... In this discourse, dildos are not substitute penises ... for these lesbians, their dildos are the 'real thing': gay male cocks. They are saying that lesbians can put on or take off these gay male cocks at will, without ever abandoning or weakening their claim to their own lesbian identities. Anna Marie Smith, 'By Women, for Women, and about Women Rules OK?'

Lesbians are choosing to play with identity, transgressing the constraints of what lesbian is supposed to mean erotically. Any sex a lesbian has is lesbian sex, no matter who has what genitals or how they come to have them. In so far as all sexuality is transitive, the Other in oneself hooking up with the Other in another creates desire, and is fuelled by not knowing who the person you are in bed with could become, or indeed who you will be in bed and what scenarios you will enact together.

I remember when I first came out as a dyke and was with this Danish, s/m, butch top who had a fantasy about being a hermaphrodite. I went through a whole problem with dicks and what they meant. I think when I was insecure about whether I was really a lesbian or not, that was when I found it difficult to wear a dick. It's a taboo and I don't know how much the power of dykes with dicks or how playing with gender roles in sex have to do with the fact that it's politically forbidden, even though it's a lot more acceptable now. This is the first time that I can have a cock, where it's not a dildo, where I can really role play. I can really be a man and so can she. It's completely amazing to me. I'm certain it's not going to be as horny sleeping with a man. They're not big enough and they're not hard enough. That's why my pictures are so threatening to straight men, because they can't compete with dildos and they know it. Della Grace

Discussion of gender expression and transgender has always taken place under a discussion of butch/femme in the US and so it has a huge impact on the lesbian movement, because actually there's a very large section of people who are lesbian, who live as men and who used to be referred to as 'he-shes' who are very, very masculine, to the point of challenging all gender boundaries in this country. And that shapes their everyday struggle in trying to find a job or use a bathroom or walk the streets or be served in a restaurant. I think also the discussions about femme women, whether or not they look like heterosexuals, are all discussions about gender. So I wrote *Stone Butch Blues* because I could see that the discussions about gender were at that high-water mark again. I wanted to show the way the lesbi/gay/bi community and the trans-community partially overlap: the drag queen and the drag king population, as well as our transsisters, transsexual brothers coming out as gay, lesbian and bi. And for those of us who are in that part that overlaps, we can see the enormous basis there is for unity, between these two huge embattled populations. Leslie Feinberg

What's interesting to me is who gets targeted in these right-wing backlashes. Traditionally, it's always women, lesbians and gays, sex workers, the rainbow of transgendered folk, s/m players. And I'm looking at what they have in common. What's important about the trangendered movement is that it supplies the missing link to what we all have in common. And that is we all break the rules of gender. Kate Bornstein

Relationships with transgendered people

Issues for the non-transgendered lesbian partners of transgendered people include coming to understand what it means for their partners to be trans-sexual or transgendered, what it means socially and how this impacts on their own identity. For people who were already in relationships when their partners began transition, there is the discovery of what the changes taking place mean in terms of relations of power, sexual chemistry, desire and sexual practices, as well as negotiations of new terms of reference which may mean challenging gender stereotypes. Other patriarchal relationship norms may emerge as roles change and as the transitioning partner sometimes overcompensates in the initial stages of the new gender role.

Difference and change, and fear of this, are just one aspect in the complex reworking of relationships. Often the non-transgendered partner has no voice, and nowhere to take fears, feelings of loss and ambivalences towards the transition, if s/he is being supportive. One of the important roles of the non-transgendered partner is validating and reflecting the transgendered partner's gender on a sexual and social level, which is critical in contributing to the acceptance of oneself as credible in one's new gender role.

I suppose what did end up concerning me, but was something I was too naive to recognise, was when I said that her transsexuality was irrelevant to me – it clearly wasn't irrelevant to her. And she was pretty well in the closet at the time, some of her closest friends didn't know. Although everybody knew she was a lesbian, not everybody knew that she was transsexual and I think it is a very natural part of a painful process of coming out to people that you always lash out at the people closest to you. I learned huge amounts, but I began to feel that I was walking on eggshells and would look to everything to see if I was doing the right thing as her reactions would be so volatile. Unfortunately, this created tremendous pressure that ultimately was a big part in the break-up of our relationship. Susan Hayward

Lesbians involved with FTMs don't necessarily become heterosexual or bisexual; in fact many keep their lesbian identities, albeit a negotiated one. Although an FTM partner's sexism or traditional masculine expectations could become a point of conflict within the relationship, with the newly reconstructed variety, the FTM New Man, it needn't take any more negotiation than a femme might have with a butch or any two lesbians might have around power differentials within their relationship. The significant difference with FTMs as social men is the way society views them as a couple and empowers him, recognising and assuming heterosexuality, even if one or both of the partners is queer. This renders the queer identities invisible while rewarding reproductions of the norm. This erasure can have a deeply eroding effect on one's sense and experience of identity.

I think a lot of it depends on how the other person defines themselves. Some people will manage to do it. But I think that the partner has to be flexible enough. It's really difficult if they consider themselves a lesbian, if they're really attached to their lesbian identity and they're involved with somebody who's calling themselves a man. David Harrison

Aaron is heterosexual and it personifies his personality. Before I met Aaron I knew that my sexuality was lesbian. My whole way of thinking was pro-woman and anti-man. I wouldn't say I was a man-hater, but I didn't like a lot of men. And being in a relationship with Aaron has made me actually deny my identity at times, because he's a man and he's with a woman and that instantly puts him into a heterosexual role. Aaron had preconceived that to be a man he had to be loud, aggressive and macho. The lesbian gets totally swamped by this maleness. It gives him a lot of power. Although he feels that he doesn't have a great deal of power because of being a transsexual and that is what he's fighting for. In being denied my identity I felt very frustrated. I felt very left out of my world, my community. I think if I were bisexual, I could accept it a lot easier. But I'm not. Kacha

I always thought of L. as a woman. I mean completely. I never thought of her as anything other than a woman, except when it came up through her own initiation of discussion around it because of problems she felt were arising. And so because I always saw her as a woman, I also saw myself completely as a lesbian. It didn't shake my identity in myself as a lesbian at all. I also see myself as a top femme, which kinda made it easier, I guess. What it did do was make me very aware of gender identity even in the smallest things, from the way you dress onwards. And role play. And that's something I still think about, in terms of positioning on an almost daily level. Susan Hayward

The 'strangeness' of transgendered genitals and sexuality can be a source of fascination and attraction for partners or, equally, can cease to hold any attraction, as when a dyke lover becomes one of the men that his lesbian partner had rejected sexually because she loved women or disliked men and penises.

Hormones contribute to the ways genitals transmute, change their form and functioning, but also affect structures in the brain (known for its plasticity) which determine sexual behaviour. There are valid questions about whether sexual behaviour or the way one wants to use one's genitals is due to new signals from the brain or is based on the new experience of the changed genitals or is simply self-fulfilling prophecy, according to those who rule out a biological reason for sex and gender behaviour.

There is of course a danger in taking these factors out of a social and ideological context, which is where the meanings of intent and subsequent behaviours remain grounded. There is perhaps a strong element of giving oneself permission for certain behaviour which one is inclined towards if it is consistent with stereotypical behaviour for the new gender role, but that's not the whole story.

I suppose all of my partners, to some extent, must have some attraction to my transsexualism, otherwise they wouldn't be with me, they'd be with a genetic woman. I am very much of Kate Bornstein's view: I'm certainly not a man, but it's debatable whether I actually am a woman. I have to live in society, so to all intents and purposes I am, but I'm transgendered. And I'm happy about being transgendered. It's all part of me. It's being loved for what I am: that's actually quite important. I actually enjoy being desired for what I am. I've been in situations where I've been desired for being a woman and someone found out that I'm transgendered and I've been rejected. I've found that really much harder to deal with. I also don't like the idea of being second best. Caroline

Aaron doesn't like me touching his breasts or nipples, and that's very hard for me. And I sort of thought, 'Once he has the mastectomy, he'll be more at

ease and he won't have to walk around with hundreds of teeshirts on.' I feel quite frustrated not being able to touch him as I would touch a woman.

I asked Aaron once, 'You have a female body, when you get aroused what happens?' He said nothing happens, he doesn't feel anything there, in his pussy. I just can't understand that concept at all. The sensation he's always had is as if he had a penis. So I thought 'Well, maybe he's a hermaphrodite.' When I saw his clitoris for the first time I thought, 'God, that looks like a little dick.' It is. It's got a little helmet. He basically does feel that it's a little penis. I wouldn't let him use a dildo because I wouldn't want any phallic instrument inside me. But he would love to be able to fuck me as a man. And he does actually. Sometimes I'm actually in tears by it. Sometimes he's very aggressive, incredibly so. And he just doesn't take time out to see that I'm upset. That is a male mentality. Men will just carry on fucking and fucking to get their rocks off and it doesn't matter who's underneath them. I can't bear that sort of mentality at all. I've talked to him, he knows it upsets me, he says, 'I'm sorry, I can't control myself sometimes.' Kacha

What makes people prone to rape? It obviously isn't testosterone, because 99 per cent of the male population are not interested in rape, are they? Rape is about power, not about testosterone. It's about violent power. Steven Whittle

Power within the relationship may be about how demanding the transgendered person is in terms of the partner getting it right. Yet outside the relationship power in society does not, ultimately, seem to reside with transgendered people but rather with those empowered to include MTFs as lesbians or not in lesbian social situations, with queer bashers in the street, or with the medical establishment which can withhold treatment for years without seeming cause. These things all impact on relationships.

The future: the postmodern lesbian body and transgender trouble

6 The cybernetic revolution, in view of the equivalence of brain and computer, places humanity before the crucial question "Am I a man or a machine?" The genetic revolution that is taking place at the moment raises the question "Am I a man or just a potential clone?" The sexual revolution, by liberating all the potentialities of desire, raises another fundamental question, "Am I a man or a woman?" (If it has done nothing else, psychoanalysis has certainly added its weight to this principle of sexual uncertainty.) ... Such is the paradoxical outcome of every revolution: revolution opens the door to indeterminacy, anxiety and confusion. Once the orgy was over, liberation was seen to have left everyone looking for their generic and sexual identity – and with fewer and fewer answers available, in view of the traffic in signs and the multiplicity of pleasures on offer. That is how we became transsexuals. 9 Jean Baudrillard, *The Transparency of Evil*

New forms: cyborgs, virtual bodies and cybergenders

Baudrillard's question – man or woman? – is reminiscent of the first question you're usually asked when you meet someone in cyberspace on the Internet. M or F (pronounced MorF)? Male or female? If you're David Harrison or Kate Bornstein, your answer would be 'Yes', much to the bafflement of the questioner.

Another of Baudrillard's questions (man or machine?) also points to the technological component of sex reassignment. In 'The Empire Strikes Back: A Posttranssexual Manifesto' Sandy Stone sees the potential of transgender in terms of Donna Haraway's 'promises of monsters – physicalities of constantly shifting figure and ground that exceed the frame of any possible representation'. These transgender monsters are cyborgs – hybrids of nature and technology, whose disruptive juxtapositions of 'the refigured body onto conventional gender discourse' create dissonances which yield 'new and unexpected geometries'.

So to this either/or, the answer is 'both'. Yes, a cyborg. And to MorF? Yes, a mighty morphing shapeshifter, who is xenomorph, third sex and trans-gendered.

In the search for new vocabularies and labels terms like 'shapeshifter' and 'morphing' have come to be used to refer to gender identity and sexual style presentations and their fluidity. 'Shapeshifter', originally from Native American culture, was introduced into current popular culture from science fiction, especially a new offshoot of the cyberpunk subgenre made famous by William Gibson and exemplified by the work of Octavia E. Butler, the African-American author of the Xenogenesis series.

Butler's books are inhabited by genetics-manipulating aliens, a polygen-dered species whose sexuality is multifarious and who are 'impelled to metamorphosis', whose survival in fact depends upon their 'morphological change, genetic diversity and adaptations'. The xenogenetic result of their mating with humans is an 'alien-human, polyracial, hybrid figure of uncertain gender' (Stephanie A. Smith, 'Morphing, Materialism, and the Marketing of Xenogenesis').

The science fiction, science fact cyborg, a cybernetic organism which is a product of the organic and technological, of human and machine, was politi-cised by Donna Haraway in, 'Cyborg Manifesto: Science, Technology, and Socialist-Feminism in the Late Twentieth Century'. Haraway argues for 'the cyborg as a fiction mapping on social and bodily reality' and that '[t]he cyborg is a creature in a postgender world' which refuses any belief in a unified identity, contesting identity politics and calling for a new 'affinity' politics of diversity and blurred boundaries.

'Morphing' is a computer special effects technique used in films and music videos, as in Michael Jackson's video 'Black or White' in which the sequential merging of images by rapid dissolves joins the faces of black and white men and women, giving the impression of a fluid, seamless metamorphosis.

Science fiction is already social fact, in that through the interventions of technology we can play with multiple, virtual identities on the Internet. You can be any gender, race or alien species, and a different one at each encounter. Also through the intervention of technology, people can modify their bodies to be what they want. In San Francisco people are talking about radical plastic surgery which could redesign the human body; for example, rearranging the muscles of the back to give yourself angel's wings, if that's what's aestheti-cally pleasing to you (David Gale, 'Cyberspaced').

So sex reassignment surgery could be seen as just another form of body modification along with piercing, branding and tattooing. Techniques are becoming more sophisticated with the advent of recombinant DNA technology.

The reason that I say it's cosmetic surgery is because people are always changing their bodies, especially in America. I suppose that if we considered what we're now calling transsexual surgery as cosmetic, maybe we would take the stigma away. Maybe we wouldn't see it as

the complete, pathological rearrangement of identity, even if it's experienced as such. Maybe we'd begin to see it as a way of organising your body to suit your image of yourself. And then we wouldn't have to have this whole therapeutic intervention, where people are saying, 'Why do you want to become a man? What's wrong with you?' You could say, 'Because I prefer the way a penis looks on my body to the way a vagina looks on my body.' Judith Halberstam

The possibility of embodying and enacting virtual identities may be the answer to the question of whether we need gender at all, transcending the issue with the existence of supernumerary genders/sexes. Technology is giving us the third space.

But can we escape gender as a category completely? Do we need gender? For some, gender is only a tool of the erotic, a way of focusing desires and attracting others. Perhaps genders/sexes could function more like language, motivated but arbitrary signs carrying desire as words do meaning but remaining only signs for our manipulation, not essential realities in themselves.

I'm writing a novel with a friend of mine, Caitlin Sullivan, about two people who meet on the Internet and have this amazing fast and furious cybersex and they start falling for each other, but they agree not to tell each other what they really are because they like having the freedom of being whatever they want to be. And they don't want to know what the other one is. And so they meet throughout the course of the book in all these different genders and ages and races and sexual combinations, you name it. And sometimes they know who the other is and sometimes they don't. But they keep falling deeper for each other. And what Caitlin came up with is this amazing simple theory. That the word 'attraction' contains the word 'traction'. And that's what you need for there to be any kind of sexuality. And then I came across this old Chinese philosopher, Chuangtzu. He said that the mouse trap exists for the purpose of the mouse. Once you've got the mouse, you don't need the trap. Words exist by reason of the meaning. Once you've got the meaning, you no longer need the words. And from that I take it that gender and identity, which I would call nearly synonymous, exist for reason of a relationship; and once you've got a relationship, you don't need a fixed identity any more. Kate Bornstein

All this deconstruction and yearning for fluidity anticipate future evolutions of social genders and physical sexes, the actual outcome of which can only be speculated about. For now, these circulating representations of new genders to come urgently reveal the limitations of our existing categories, although our lives are already creating queer dissonances and unexpected geo-metrical combinations.

The end of identity in this gender fiction does not mean a limitless and boundless shifting of positions and forms; rather it indicates the futility of stretching terms like lesbian or gay or straight or male or female across vast fields of experience, behaviour and self-understanding. It further hints at the inevitable exclusivity of any claim to identity and refuses the respectability of being named, identified, known. Judith Halberstam, 'F2M'

As it took centuries for the one-sex model of antiquity to give way to the two-sex model of post-Enlightenment, so the vestiges of the nineteenth-century model of sex and gender persist even as competing models emerge on the eve of the twenty-first century.

Post-transsexual: the empire strikes back

This aspiration towards a third sex is far more common than transsexual stereotypes would seem to suggest ... Transsexuals want to belong to the sex of the angels. Catherine Millot, *Horsexe*

I think we all already are transgendered. And I think the focus on what are called popularly transgendered people today is the tip of the iceberg pointing to what already exists. Kate Bornstein

Everyone performs their gender as a matter of course. The gender bending, gender fuck and shapeshifting behaviour of some queer people is a subversive expression of this capacity. Living as feminine men and masculine women and exhibiting gender 'inappropriate' behaviour comprise a tradition in the gay community. Cross-dressing and cross-gendered behaviour, whether with the assistance of technology or not, places people somewhere among a range of gender identities, behaviours and styles along the continuum.

Third sex/gender does not imply a single expression or an androgynous mixing, comically characterised by Mary Daly as 'scotch-taping John Wayne and Brigitte Bardot together' (Daly, 'The Qualitative Leap'). The third gender category is a space for society to articulate and make sense of all its various gendered identities, as more people refuse to continue to hide them or remain silent on the margins.

Because I was struggling to find my identity, discovering it is just such an amazing feeling. I think that people are too easily pigeon-holed into being one thing or another. I had to come out and say I was something that most people couldn't even accept existed. At the time I'd never heard of it myself. I just knew that it had to be right, which was difficult to do. I think that people should push back the boundaries more and be more prepared to explore and accept rather than just be pigeon-holed into something just because it feels safe or what they're familiar with. Christie Elan-Cane

If more transsexual people were able to identify as transgendered and express their third gender category status, instead of feeling forced to slot into the binary because of the threats of punishment and loss of social legitimacy, that third category would be far more peopled than one might imagine. People could be given legitimacy by this third category, if society recognised gender diversity alongside ethnic or religious diversity. And, as with cultures contiguous to ours, that operate within a multigendered paradigm, Western culture would be significantly enriched by the contributions of people with these unique experiences.

As Kate Bornstein says, visible transgendered people are just the tip of the iceberg. Of course this is threatening to the patriarchy and the heterosexual imperative, because multiple genders would signal an end to the myth of male gender supremacy and the material consequences of male domination. Third sex/gender people have been a lost tribe to Western culture.

Sandy Stone argues that the essence of transsexualism is the act of passing and that to deconstruct the necessity of passing implies taking responsibility for all of one's history, to enrich and empower one's life. It is resisting the monolithic foreclosure of gender identity.

I could not ask a transsexual for anything more inconceivable than to forgo passing, to be consciously 'read', to read oneself aloud – and by this troubling and productive reading, to begin to write oneself into the discourse by which one has been written – in effect, then, to become ... posttranssexual. Sandy Stone, 'The Empire Strikes Back'

A word of warning to the 'monomorphs': the transgender menace is among you and we recruit!

Postmodern lesbian

Our categories are important. We cannot organize a social life, political movement, or our individual identities and desires without them. The fact that categories invariably leak and can never contain all the relevant 'existing things' does not render them useless, only limited. Categories like 'woman', 'butch', 'lesbian', or 'transsexual' are all imperfect, historical, temporary, and arbitrary. Instead of fighting for immaculate classifications and impenetrable boundaries, let us strive to maintain a community that understands diversity as a gift, sees anomalies as precious, and treats all basic principles with a hefty dose of scepticism. Gayle Rubin, 'Of Catamites and Kings'

I've stopped calling myself a lesbian, simply because the rock bottom, most agreed upon definition of lesbians is women who love women. I don't call myself a woman, so I'm not a lesbian. That doesn't change my sexual orientation towards people who do define themselves as women or mostly as not men. I think that it's important for the time being that lesbian exists as a category because it is such a dangerous category, because it says we can live very well without men, thank you

very much. And I personally don't want to rock that boat at this time in our joint struggles. I would say I can call myself a dyke because that seems to include lesbians but goes into a less holy space, a less restrictive space that includes transgendered people. Kate Bornstein

The increased visibility of transgender in the lesbian community, like s/m and other variations on gender, sexuality and sexual practices, continues to impress on us the fact that 'sex between two genetic females, acting as women' (as Judith Halberstam puts it) is perhaps now the more marginal lesbian sex practice. There are fewer lesbians choosing to express their gender and sexuality in the mould of the lesbian category as it has been represented for the past two decades. Lesbian feminist fundamentalism no longer speaks for or to the grassroots lesbian experience.

I think that the postmodern lesbian will just disintegrate; I'm not sure that the category lesbian is going to be so important. One thing that I'm hoping for is a kind of happy alliance between lesbian communities and gender communities. Personally, I rarely identify as lesbian any more. I identify as queer. And queer just feels much better to me than lesbian because lesbian for me brings up the idea of two women being women together. And that's not me. When I'm with a woman, I'm really not being a woman. So for me the postmodern lesbian is like the withering away of lesbianism. I think we're going to have to use homosexual and heterosexual to identify whether people are interested in sameness or difference erotically. Hopefully that binary will disintegrate and open up to many other forms of identifying what you are sexually interested in. Judith Halberstam

There are already points of contact, overlaps and alliances between lesbians and transgendered people. As categories emerge and evolve and boundaries shift, those alliances will strengthen even as the categories man, woman, lesbian, gay and transsexual themselves eventually dissolve to yield different forms in the future.

In the meantime, the lesbian category is still dangerous and has a powerful function in the subversion of patriarchal social structures, perhaps even more in its postmodern form than in its radical feminist one, in that the category is being dismantled and expanded instead of entrenched and reified. The issue is no longer simply one of proving that lesbians exist as an identity, as that lesbians have common cause with other category-disrupting subversives. Part of the political potential of postmodern lesbianism is its affinity with Others, and that mutual recognition fuels and empowers lesbians to act alongside these allies to change gender in Western society: radically, fundamentally and irrevocably. The ongoing contestation and deconstruction of the monolithic gender system and the politicisation of the third gender category means that there will no longer be transsexuals and that lesbians as we know them will also cease to exist.

Bibliography

American Psychiatric Association, 'Diagnostic Criteria for 302.50, Transsexualism' in *Diagnostic and Statistical Manual of Mental Disorders*, revised 3rd edn., Washington, DC, American Psychiatric Association, 1987

Baudrillard, Jean, *The Transparency of Evil: Essays on Extreme Phenomena*, London, Verso, 1993

de Beauvoir, Simone, *The Second Sex*, New York, Bantam, 1953

Benjamin, Harry, *The Transsexual Phenomenon*, New York, Julian Press, 1966

Bolin, Anne, 'Transcending and Transgendering: Male-to-Female Transsexuals, Dichotomy and Diversity' in Herdt, G., ed., *Third Sex, Third Gender: Beyond Sexual Dimorphism in Culture and History*, New York, Zone Books, 1994

Bornstein, Kate, *Gender Outlaw: On Men, Women and the Rest of Us*, New York, Routledge, 1994

Bruce-Pratt, Minnie, *S/He*, Ithaca, NY, Firebrand, 1995

Bullough, Vern L. and Bullough, Bonnie, *Cross Dressing, Sex, and Gender*, Philadelphia, University of Pennsylvania Press, 1993

Butler, Judith, *Gender Trouble: Feminism and the Subversion of Identity*, New York, Routledge, 1990

Califia, Pat, 'Who is my Sister? Powersurge and the Limits of our Community', *venus infers*, 1(1), 1993

Clare, D. and Tully, B., 'Transhomosexuality, or the Dissociation of Sexual Orientation and Sex Object Choice', *Archives of Sexual Behavior*, 18, 1989

Connell, R.W., *Gender and Power: Society, the Person, and Sexual Politics*, Stanford, CA, Stanford University Press, 1987

Cossey, Caroline, *My Story*, Winchester, Faber and Faber, 1992

Daly, Mary, 'The Qualitative Leap Beyond Patriarchal Religion', *Quest: A Feminist Quarterly*, 1, Spring 1975

Devor, Holly, 'Sexual Orientation Identities, Attractions, and Practices of Female-to-Male Transsexuals', *Journal of Sex Research*, 30(4), November 1993

Diamond, Milton, 'Human Sexual Development: Biological Foundations for Social Development', in *Human Sexuality in Four Perspectives*, ed. Beach, Frank, Baltimore, MD, Johns Hopkins Press, 1977

Elliott, Beth, 'AND? AND? AND? A Stonewall for the Rest of Us', *Transsexual News Telegraph*, 3, summer 1994

Feinberg, L. *Stone Butch Blues*, Ithaca, NY, Firebrand, 1993

Findlay, Heather, 'Modern Stone: What is Stone Butch – Now ?', *Girlfriend*, 2(2), March/April 1995

Foucault, Michel, introduction to *Herculine Barbin: Being the Recently Discovered Memoirs of a Nineteenth-Century French Hermaphrodite*, trans.

Richard McDougall, New York, Pantheon, 1980

Gale, David, 'Cyberspaced', GQ, December 1993

Garber, Marjorie, Vested Interests: Cross-Dressing and Cultural Anxiety, London, Routledge, 1992

Grimm, D., 'Toward a Theory of Gender: Transsexualism, Gender, Sexuality, and Relationships', American Behavioral Scientist, 31, 1987

Halberstam, Judith, 'F2M: The Making of Female Masculinity', in Doan, Laura, ed., The Lesbian Postmodern, New York, Columbia University Press, 1994

Haraway, Donna, 'Cyborg Manifesto: Science, Technology, and Socialist-Feminism in the Late Twentieth Century' in Haraway, Simians, Cyborgs, and Women: The Reinvention of Nature, London, Free Association, 1991

Hodgkinson, Liz, Michael, Neé Laura: The Story of the World's First Female-to-Male Transsexual, London, Columbus, 1989

Horwitz, Kevin, 'The Art of Passing', Transsexual News Telegraph, winter 1994

Hoyer, Niels, ed., with Elbe, Lili, Man into Woman: An Authentic Record of a Change of Sex. The True Story of the Miraculous Transformation of the Danish Painter, Einar Wegener, trans. Stenning, H.J., New York, E.P. Dutton, 1933

Jeffreys, Sheila, Anticlimax: Feminist Perspective on the Sexual Revolution, London, The Women's Press, 1990

Jorgensen, Christine, A Personal Autobiography, New York, Paul S. Eriksson, 1967

Kessler, Suzanne J. and McKenna, Wendy, Gender: An Ethnomethodological Approach, New York, Wiley, 1978

Krafft-Ebing, Richard von, Psychopathia Sexualis: With Especial Reference to the Antipathic Sexual Instinct: A Medico-Forensic Study, trans. Rebman, F.J., New York, Physicians & Surgeons Book Co. [1906] 1933; originally published in German 1886

Laqueur, Thomas, Making Sex: Body and Gender from the Greeks to Freud, Cambridge, MA, Harvard University Press, 1990

LeVay, Simon, The Sexual Brain, Cambridge, MA, MIT Press, 1993

Millot, Catherine, Horsexe: Essay on Transsexuality, Brooklyn, NY, Autonomedia, 1990

Money, John, 'Transsexualism and Homosexuality in Sanskrit: 2.5 Millennia of Ayurvedic Sexology', Gender Dysphoria, 1(2), 1992

Morris, Jan, Conundrum: An Extraordinary Narrative of Transsexualism, New York, Harcourt Brace Jovanovich, 1974

Nanda, Serena, Neither Man nor Woman: The Hijras of India, Belmont, CA, Wordsworth, 1990

——, 'Hijras: An Alternative Sex and Gender Role in India' in Herdt, G., ed., Third Sex, Third Gender: Beyond Sexual Dimorphism in Culture and History, New York, Zone Books, 1994

O'Donovan, Katherine, 'Transsexual Troubles: The Discrepancy between Legal and Social Categories', in Edwards, Susan, ed., Gender, Sex and the Law, London, Croom Helm, 1985

Raymond, Janice G., *The Transsexual Empire*, Boston, MA, Beacon, 1979

Reynolds Nangeroni, Nancy, 'Gender Outlaws: Kate Bornstein and David Harrison', *TV/TS Tapestry Journal*, 68, summer 1994

Richards, Renée and Ames, John, *Second Serve: The Renée Richards Story*, New York, Stein & Day, 1983

Roscoe, Will, 'How to Become a Berdache: Toward a Unified Analysis of Gender Diversity', in Herdt, G., ed., *Third Sex, Third Gender: Beyond Sexual Dimorphism in Culture and History*, New York, Zone Books, 1994

Rothblatt, Martine Aliana, *The Apartheid of Sex: A Manifesto on the Freedom of Gender*, New York, Crown, 1995

Rubin, Gayle, 'Of Catamites and Kings: Reflections on Butch, Gender, and Boundaries', in Nestle, Joan, ed., *The Persistent Desire: A Femme-Butch Reader*, Boston, MA, Alyson, 1992

Shapiro, Judith, 'Transsexualism: Reflections on the Persistence of Gender and the Mutability of Sex', in Epstein, J., and Straub, K., eds, *Body Guards*, New York, Routledge, 1991

Smith, Anna Marie, '"By Women, for Women and about Women" Rules OK? The Impossibility of Visual Soliloquy', in Burston, Paul and Richardson, Colin, eds, *A Queer Romance*, London, Routledge, 1995

Smith, Stephanie A., 'Morphing, Materialism, and the Marketing of Xenogenesis', *Genders*, 18, winter 1993

Steinke, Darcy, *Suicide Blonde*, London, Picador, 1993

Stone, Sandy, 'The Empire Strikes Back: A Posttranssexual Manifesto', in Epstein, J. and Straub, K., ed., *Body Guards*, New York, Routledge, 1991

Stuart, K.E., *The Uninvited Dilemma: A Question of Gender*, Portland, OR, Metamorphous, 1991

Sullivan, Louis, *From Female to Male: The Life of Jack Bee Garland*, Boston, MA, Alyson, 1990

Swaab and Hofman, 'Sexual Differentiation of the Human Hypothalamus in Relation to Gender and Sexual Orientation', *Trends in Neurosciences*, 18(6), 1995

Swan, Susan, *The Wives of Bath*, London, Granta/Penguin, 1993

Waddington, Aimée, 'Herms, Ferms, Merms and the Biopower of the Surgical Shoehorn: A Critical Review of Anne Fausto-Sterling, "The Five Sexes: Why Male and Female are Not Enough", (*Sciences*, March/April 1993)', *Dyscourse*, 5(4), July/August 1993

Walker, Paul A. (Chairperson, Harry Benjamin International Gender Dysphoria Association) with Berger, J.C., Green, R., Laub, D.R., Reynolds, C.L., Jr., Wollman, L., *Standards of Care: The Hormonal and Surgical Sex Reassignment of Gender Dysphoric Persons*, Galveston, TX, Janus Information Facility, University of Texas Medical Branch, 1979 (revised edn. 1990)

Glossary

assigned gender at birth – gender one is considered to be at birth, based on external sex organs

bigendered – those who feel they have both a male and a female side to their personalities

cross-dresser (CD) – someone who from time to time wears the clothes of the opposite (of their physical anatomical) gender, to relieve gender discomfort. Cross-dressers want to appear as 'convincing' as possible as their other selves. This term is preferable to 'transvestite'

cross-living – living fulltime in the preferred gender image, opposite to one's assigned sex at birth, generally in preparation for a sex-change operation

drag – originally used [1] in Shakespeare's Globe Theatre to mean DRessed As Girl, referring to male actors playing female roles. Now [2] mainly used by gender benders and cross-dressers of both directions to mean 'in women's clothes'. Less frequently used, **drab** means DRessed As Boy

drag king – FTM cross-dresser, often **packing** (see)

drag queen – gay man who from time to time wears women's clothes, generally without attempting to be 'convincing'

gender bender – anyone crossing the gender line who does not care about appearing 'convincing'. Also **gender fuck** – politicised cross-dressing, in both directions, emphasising gender ambiguity and challenging traditional gender concepts

gender dysphoria – being unhappy with the assigned (anatomical) gender. Fullblown gender dysphoria syndrome is the same as **transsexualism**

genetic – [1] refers to the chromosomal endowment of the individual (sex chromosomes XX in women and XY in men). [2] someone who is not transgendered, e.g. genetic male

he-she – extremely masculine, cross-dressing women, who often **pass** (see); frequently butch lesbians; also **drag king** (see), bull-dagger (BD), gender blender

intersex – born with the (full or partial) sex organs of both anatomical genders or with underdeveloped or ambiguous sex organs. (Replaces the politically incorrect terms hermaphrodite and pseudo-hermaphrodite)

packing – wearing a dildo or penile prosthesis

pass – to be in your preferred gender image, and to be able to do so convincingly

read – when someone detects you are transgendered; also clock(ed)

she-male – MTF cross-dresser with 'tits, big hair, lots of make-up and a dick' (Bornstein) Also 'chick with a dick', she-hes, **transgenderist** (see)

transgender (TG) – originally [1] what are also known as fulltime cross-dressers or non-surgical transsexuals, people who live and work in the opposite (of their physical anatomical) gender continuously (see **transgenderist**). Now it also means [2] the group of *all* people who are inclined to cross the gender line. Sometimes used [3] as a synonym for **transsexual** (see)

transgenderist – same as definition [1] of transgender, used to avoid confusion

transphobia – the groundless fear and hatred of cross-dressers, transsexuals and gender benders and what they do, resulting in denial of rights and needs, and violence. Contrast 'T-friendly' – any organisation or institution that is accepting of transgendered peoples and their needs

transsexual (TS) – anyone who [1] wants to have or [2] has had, a sex-change operation, including [3] non-surgical transsexuals. TSs want to appear 'convincing' in their new roles

Part of this glossary is taken from the *Glossary of Gender* compiled by Transgender Nation, San Francisco, and is reproduced here with the kind permission of Christine Tayleur.

Contacts

BM Androgyne, London WC1N 3XX, third gender contact; send SAE

FTM, 5337 College Avenue, no. 142, Oakland, CA 94618, USA

FTM Network, BM Network, London WC1N 3XX

Gender Identity Consultancy Services (formerly the **Gender Dysphoria Trust International**), BM Box 5434, London WC1N 3XX; tel. (01323) 470230

Gender Team Amsterdam, /VU, De Boelclaan 1117, 1008 HV Amsterdam, Netherlands; tel. (31)(20)5489111, ext. 199

Gender Trust, The, or **GEMS**, BM Gentrust, London WC1N 3XX; tel. (01305) 269222, before 10 pm

Intersex Society of North America, PO Box 31791, San Francisco, CA 94131, USA

National Council for Civil Liberties (Liberty), 21 Tabard Street, London SE1 4LA; tel. 0171-4033888

Press For Change, BM Network, London WC1N 3XX

Transgender Nation, 370 Monterey Blvd., Suite no. 201, San Fransisco, CA 94131-3150

Transsexual Menace, c/o Gender Identity Project, The Lesbian & Gay Community Services Center, 208 West 13th Street, New York, New York 10011; tel. (212) 6207310

Internet news groups

transgen@brownum.brown.edu-email:-subscribe transgen (your name), send to listserv-@brownum.brown.edu

alt.transgendered – conference notices, factual information, comment and questions

World Wide Web [WWW] sites

http://rniles.pnw.net/transgen.html – transgender resource site

http://www.ftm-intl.org – American FTM group organised by James Green of FTM, California

UK contact

100275.2265@compuserve.com or **s.t.whittle@mmu.ac.uk** – FTM Network